Rapid Development
with
Oracle CASE

Rapid Development
with
Oracle CASE

A Workshop Approach

Chris & Maria Billings

Addison-Wesley Publishing Company

Reading, Massachusetts Menlo Park, California New York
Don Mills, Ontario Wokingham, England Amsterdam Bonn
Sydney Singapore Tokyo Madrid San Juan Paris
Seoul Milan Mexico City Taipei

The publisher offers discounts on this book when ordered in quantity for special sales. For more information please contact:

Corporate & Professional Publishing Group
Addison-Wesley Publishing Company
One Jacob Way
Reading, Massachusetts 01867

Library of Congress Cataloging-in-Publication Data

Billings, Chris.
  Rapid development with Oracle CASE: a workshop approach/Chris Billings and Maria Billings.
    p. cm.
  ISBN 0-201-63344-2
    1. Computer software—Development. 2. Oracle (Computer file)
I. Billings, Maria. II. Title.
QA76.76.D47B55   1993
005.75'6—dc20   93-8205
                                                        CIP

Every effort has been made to supply accurate information. However, the authors do not warrant that this document is error-free.

ORACLE, CASE*Dictionary, CASE*Designer, SQL*DBA, SQL*Forms, SQL*Menu, SQL*Plus, and SQL*ReportWriter are registered trademarks; CASE*Generator, SQL*TextRetrieval, Oracle*Terminal, ORACLE7, and Oracle Graphics are trademarks; and CASE*Method and CASE*Workshops are service marks of Oracle Corporation.

OS/2 is a trademark of International Business Machines.

All other names and products appearing in this book are trademarks of their respective companies.

Text design by Melissa A. Kulig
Set in 10-point Times by GEX Publishing Services, Inc.
Text printed on recycled and acid-free paper.

3 4 5 6 7 8 9 10-CRW-97969594
Third printing, December 1994

Contents

Foreword

Here is a book that combines the power of Computer-Aided Systems Engineering (CASE) with the practicality of expert consulting, fueled by the need to achieve rapid results in a workshop or pilot project environment.

This hands-on guide to CASE is intended for anyone interested in a dynamic approach to developing robust information systems, and especially for those who have selected or are considering Oracle Corporation's family of tools for CASE. The workshop style comes from Oracle's proof-of-concept approach to CASE—a key to understanding and demonstrating where the benefits of CASE actually lie.

The American market for CASE has come a long way from the time when the project leader could announce to his or her programmers, "You just start coding, and I'll go out and find out what they need!" Involving users in gathering requirements, rapid but careful modeling for feedback, and iterative prototyping through the use of screen and report generators are techniques now familiar to many development shops. Breakthroughs in reverse and reengineering of applications have contributed to the value of CASE technology. But no one has published a readable, practical guide on how best to apply such productivity tools in the real world—until now.

The CASE*Workshop program was piloted by Oracle USA in 1990 to show the commonsense strengths of its analysis and design methods and the rapid, flexible techniques of its application development tools. These workshop methods are now being translated into numerous other consulting houses throughout the world. The information engineering techniques that introduced structured planning and analysis into many American shops in the 1980s did improve the quality of resulting systems. This top-down approach, combined with new iterative techniques for accelerated results, is being taken up with spirit in England, Europe, and Australia. The software market has matured to cater to these new faster, more flexible methods; vendors who lack automatic generation and reengineering features are hastening to add them. Completeness and integration of tools for a best development environment have never been more important, as Oracle's increasing market share for these tools indicates.

This book demonstrates how to use CASE for rapid systems development. Part methods tutorial, part project advisor, part reference cheat-sheet, it puts the essentials into the hands of readers about to embark on a pilot CASE project, ensuring their safety.

Effective technology transfer is still a rare experience. This book is unique in making the path to CASE less complex and esoteric. The authors are experts in maximizing a company's return on investment through successful training in newly adopted software technologies. Productivity gains can only really arrive after just this kind of expert skills transfer (combined with tools that don't get in your way).

Welcome to some of the best help you are ever likely to meet.

Renée Taylor
Director, CASE Consulting Division
Oracle Corporation USA

Preface

This is a book about means—both manual and computerized—for managing the increasingly complex process of developing application software, especially in an ORACLE environment. Such methods and tools are generically classified under the heading of CASE: Computer-Aided Systems (or Software) Engineering. CASE tools are now available in a perplexing array of shapes and sizes, and the term "CASE" has become one of the primary buzz-words in the world of information systems (IS) development. These last two facts point to a third: that the IS industry is trying to cope with totally unprecedented rates of change in both hardware and software technology as well as in the ever-more-sophisticated ways that organizations choose to apply those advances. As a result, the effective use of CASE methods and tools to optimize the benefits of these changes has become critical.

Oracle Corporation is now the third largest software company in the world. This remarkable feat has been accomplished in part because Oracle chose, many years ago, to develop a relational database management system (RDBMS) that would operate on virtually every significant hardware platform in the world. And they have succeeded.

Many large organizations now find themselves with computer systems from a variety of manufacturers, all containing their own databases and, usually, their own data formats that are practically inaccessible to one another. Oracle's RDBMS and connectivity tools integrate those different systems and make their collective data accessible to users across the entire enterprise. Additionally, Oracle provides state-of-the-art application development tools for optimizing the use of this integrated information, now combined as the Cooperative Development Environment (CDE).

Taking into account Oracle's achievements in mastering the labyrinthine complexities of data and process integration, it's no surprise that their CASE tools are of a corresponding quality. In fact, Oracle's CASE is so powerful and so comprehensive that these attributes actually lead to a peculiar problem.

Organizations often acquire integrated CASE toolsets with dreams of streamlined, centrally controlled IS development based on accurate models of data and processes along with automatic, repository-driven systems generation. Then they discover how much expertise is required right at the outset—that they need analysts who understand the methods behind the tools and can form a strategy for their proper use. As a result, CASE tools are frequently underutilized, mishandled, or simply left on the shelf. Worse, the truly remarkable benefits of CASE are lost and systems continue to go into production below standard.

As CASE consultants, we've been observing this unfortunate scenario for some time. Oracle Corporation's CASE*Workshop concept was the basis upon which we began formulating our own workshop approach—specifically with the aim of providing a rapid technology transfer to clients, along with a working application that could spur interest in and commitment to more extensive use of CASE by their organization.

To do this, we needed to carry the workshop idea a step further. Rather than using standardized system specifications as a basis on which to apply the methods and tools, we wanted to speak with the client beforehand and select a functional area of their enterprise that could be taken from analysis through implementation, ideally in the course of a two-week workshop. Besides allowing participants to work with Oracle's CASE tools in a framework of familiar processes and information requirements, this method would also deliver a sample database and application specific to their needs.

This book is a result of developing and refining the CASE workshop concept. It can be used by consultants as a model for carrying out their own workshops. But perhaps more importantly, it can serve as a fastpath tour through Oracle's CASE tools, showing step by step what actually has to be done to get the most out of these products. We sincerely hope that the book proves as useful for others to read as it has been for us to think about and to write.

We are very grateful to Renée Taylor for her investment of valuable time and support to our project. We would also like to thank our technical editors, especially Liz Johnson and Vicki Morris, both from the Oracle CASE USA staff, for their highly professional contributions, which have significantly added to the quality of this book.

1

Introduction

We begin by specifying some objectives and briefly describing the topics to be covered. Next comes some general background on the history of CASE followed by an overview of Oracle's CASE*Method. Finally, we provide a timeline for a typical ten-day CASE workshop as we would conduct it.

1.1   Aims of This Book

In creating this guide, we aim to address two very interconnected objectives. On the one hand, we intend to demonstrate how a workshop approach can greatly assist information systems (IS) professionals in familiarizing themselves with Oracle Corporation's Computer-Aided Systems Engineering (CASE) products. To do this, we pursue our second goal of taking readers on a "fastpath" through the rather complex tools and techniques involved in completing an Oracle CASE project.

Perhaps the primary reason CASE products have been given a somewhat mixed reception by the IS community is the steep learning curve required to employ fully integrated CASE (I-CASE) tool sets. This obstacle to gaining proficiency either leaves acquired CASE methods and techniques "on the shelf," or causes them to be under-utilized by inexperienced analysts, resulting in lacklustre benefits to the organizations that need them.

To overcome this problem, we find that a workshop offers the best setting in which to carry out an efficient CASE technology transfer. By gaining hands-on experience in relation to a small test project, participants are able to view the intricate web of CASE methods and tools as a working whole, a perspective no conventional training course can provide.

In our workshop environment, we study a small functional area of a real business (somewhat modified for our purposes). We start with a look at how to conduct an enterprise-wide strategy study. Then we focus on the selected scope of our project and carry out an analysis, design, and implementation of one application.

Here are some of the topics we cover:

- how specifications are gathered in CASE*Dictionary and which ones are most important for subsequent design and implementation;

- how to use CASE*Designer to model business requirements and how to use these models as communications tools and blueprints for subsequent automated designs;

- how to use CASE*Dictionary's transformation utilities;

- practical tips on conducting user interviews, group presentations, and feedback sessions; and

- how to use the CASE generators to create SQL*Forms, SQL*Plus, SQL*ReportWriter, and SQL*Menu applications generated entirely from specifications in CASE*Dictionary.

So that the book can encompass a wider variety of issues, we have expanded the scope of our workshop beyond what could practically be dealt with in ten working days, our usual time frame. What we lose in credibility as storytellers we hope to have gained in richness of detail and examples that can be used by a wide audience.

In dealing with as sophisticated a toolset as Oracle's CASE products, this guide assumes a certain amount of prior knowledge. Readers should be familiar with the ORACLE RDBMS and with relational database design. Some knowledge of entity and function modeling as well as SQL*Plus, SQL*Forms, SQL*Menu, and SQL*ReportWriter is also beneficial. Wherever we can, we try to pass along tips and suggestions with regard to modeling techniques, but we do not intend to provide a complete exposition of such a complex subject (see Section 5.13 for some excellent resource texts on Oracle CASE modeling). It must also be noted that true proficiency in Oracle's CASE tools can only result from the repeated exercise of analytical skills in the arena of real-world CASE projects. In our workshop environment, we attempt to simulate that arena as closely as possible.

1.2   A Little Background

CASE is a term of increasing significance for anyone who needs powerful and effective information systems. Oracle Corporation provides the ORACLE Relational Database Management System (RDBMS), which is accompanied by a complete set of integrated application development tools, including CASE products.

The emergence of CASE in the last decade is probably a sign that IS development is coming of age. This maturation process really began with the introduction of structured programming techniques in the early 1970s. These principles provided an important first step toward establishing standards by which the quality of a software development process could be judged. But structured programming could not truly address the more serious challenges as new computer technologies continued to broaden the range of possible applications. These issues have become especially apparent in the world of large corporations with their need for complex, distributed, and frequently global information systems. Sophisticated structures require a flexible yet tightly managed environment both for their development and maintenance. Just as highly complex engineering projects have long been controlled by rigorous tools for analysis and cross-checking, so are IS applications now coming under similar scrutiny.

When structured methods and then CASE tools appeared on the scene, many recognized them as a much-needed antidote to the increasingly unmanageable character of large-scale IS projects. Unfortunately, early enthusiasm tended to be more pronounced among high-level executives, those who stood to lose the most when projects failed. The people who would be applying these tools, the analysts and designers themselves, were often more reluctant.

Even one of the authors, upon first attending a CASE seminar, was initially put off by the meticulous cross-checking techniques that CASE uses to be effective. His objection was something on the order of: "Why should I be subjected to all this nit-picking? I've spent years developing intuitive skills that speed up and even guarantee a successful project without any of this!" But such objections come from those who have seen the price tag without the product or its benefits. This attitude is valid only for very small, stand-alone projects: as soon as the scale expands and/or the complexity increases, project management becomes more serious and CASE becomes crucial.

Of course, full participation in any new approach is difficult until we're convinced of its value. Yet the application of CASE tools is no different from the use of any sophisticated technique designed to enhance the skills of a master. At the same time, it's no "silver bullet," and buying a tool is not a substitute for skilled and thorough analysis. The biggest obstacle to the practical application of Oracle CASE generally comes right up front: it is the threat presented by an apparent labyrinth of screens, diagrams, and reports that are actually designed to make our work simpler, not more complex. The recognition of this problem was the original impetus for conducting CASE workshops.

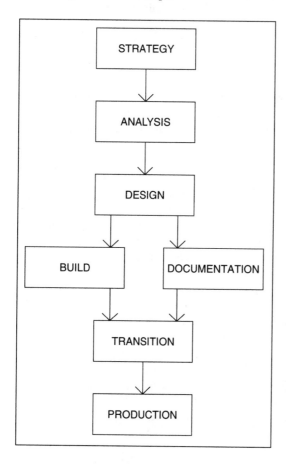

Figure 1.1
Business System Life Cycle

Despite its sophistication and complexity, Oracle's I-CASE development environment is now so efficient that software houses maintaining customized applications for several clients often use CASE*Dictionary and the CASE generators to develop and store templates with a "look-and-feel" and tailoring particular to each product sold.

So how are best results achieved? What does CASE actually do? Since this book is devoted to answering such questions, we make this introduction to CASE a brief one. Richard Barker, the senior vice president of Oracle Corporation responsible for developing CASE, provides a useful definition. He calls CASE "a staged approach to methodically engineer a business system by following a prescribed life-cycle." The stages that Oracle uses are described in the "Business System Life Cycle" (see Fig. 1.1). In the limited time frame of our workshop, we are able to produce only a subset of all the deliverables required from a complete CASE study. But what follows is an overview of that process, when carried out in its entirety and in an Oracle CASE environment.

Strategy

A well-conducted strategy study that defines an organization's directions and requirements greatly increases the likelihood that subsequent systems development will meet those critical objectives. First it is necessary to establish exactly what those primary objectives and directions are. Then the information needs can be analyzed. These strategic data are gained primarily through interviews with senior management. The consultants' job is to organize the resulting information in such a way that they can return to interviewees in iterative "feedback sessions" with various reconstructed models of the organization until everyone involved is satisfied with their accuracy. CASE*Dictionary not only allows us to store models of an organization's functions, processes, and data requirements, but also serves as a repository for information on objectives, priorities, critical success factors, key performance indicators, and even objects that a company deems significant, outside the CASE object set, using repository extensibility.

The two modeling techniques used most often in the strategy stage are entity relationship diagrams (ERDs) and function hierarchies. An *entity* can be defined as an object (or thing) about which an organization wishes to hold information. So an ERD describes entities and the relationships between them in a manner that allows us to visualize an organization's data structure. At the strategy stage, ERDs tend to be high level in scope, providing an overview that senior management can confirm without excessive consideration of detail.

Mirroring this data model is the high-level function hierarchy. Together, these two components comprise the key strategy-stage deliverables. Starting at its top, a box is displayed with a brief mission statement. Beneath this, in a parent-child hierarchy, the various functional areas of the organization are listed. These should not be confused with departments on an "org chart": they are meant to indicate logically divisible functions of the organization, some of which might span several departments. These areas are likewise "decomposed" into a subset of functions that generally describe the tasks performed within that particular area. Later, during analysis, this model (as well as the high-level ERD) will be extended into much more detail on the level of each functional area being studied.

At the end of the strategy stage, analysts present a report with recommendations to senior management. This document is based on the preceding business analysis, and it includes a discussion of objectives, priorities, critical success factors, key performance indicators, and business constraints (such as cost issues and available resources), along with the CASE models, which by this time are stored in CASE*Dictionary awaiting more detailed analysis. The consultants also recommend alternative routes toward that analysis, as well as the subsequent design and implementation of one or more required applications. These are prioritized, again on the basis of strategic feedback. The overall project plan always needs a specific schedule for the next stage while those stages further in the future can be estimated more globally.

Analysis

Once agreement has been reached on which functional areas should be treated first, a detailed analysis of their processes and information requirements can be carried out. The cycle of interiewing and feedback sessions that was begun with senior management during strategy is now continued at a deeper level. Consultants begin by speaking with those responsible for the various areas within the project's scope. This time their aim is to arrive at detailed specifications leading to the design of a database and application.

ERDs and function hierarchies are refined and extended, including ever more specific information. The ERD that is finally arrived at by the end of analysis should, as much as possible, reflect essential business entities and relationships irrespective of limitations caused by current technologies or resource constraints (e.g., lack of funds). This way, it will continue to be a faithful data model despite changes in such circumstances. Each entity should also be accompanied by complete definitions of its attributes and relationships, and these should be "normalized," a step that ensures the proper structure of the database soon to be designed.

The function hierarchy needs to be decomposed to the level of elementary functions—processes that are complete in themselves and that actually produce new information of value. The more accurately this final decomposition is achieved, the better the application design will be.

Dataflow diagrams can also be used to chart the movement of information across processes. This technique is not required by CASE*Method but is often used, especially by developers with a third-generation programming background. Dataflow diagrams do provide one perspective needed in business analysis: a means for better understanding complex flows of data from sources external to the functional area being studied.

Utilities are now executed that establish connections from functions to entities and attributes. This allows cross-checking to be performed, either by using CASE*Designer's matrices or directly in CASE*Dictionary. One important cross-check relates elementary functions to the entities they use, and a major task during analysis is to refine these usages. This will prove most valuable in the next stage, during application design. Another useful matrix relates business units to elementary functions, thus building a basis from which access control to the application can be developed.

While the data and process analysis is going on, the consultants need to be planning the often complex transition of their application into production use as well as ascertaining the security requirements. But the primary deliverable from this analysis is a complete set of specifications, including complete data and function models and their associated usages. These must be agreed upon by the sponsoring user, for the design both of a database and application. Presentation of this material is made much easier by CASE*Dictionary's wide range of reports.

Design

Two questions that should have been dealt with by the end of the analysis stage concern distributed systems: are they required and what exactly needs to be distributed? The answers to these have an impact on many of the issues that follow. They are part of defining the hardware and software environments for production, but the systems to be used for development and testing must also be established. Details such as types of equipment, networks (their protocol and bandwidth), operating systems, national languages, and character sets can be critical constraints on the project. To design for good performance, it is necessary to know the tools at hand. Similarly, programming standards and conventions need to be established, not only for the original building of the application but also with its portability and maintenance in mind. To inform end users of the various possibilities open to them as well as to begin establishing the desired look and feel of the application, prototyping can be a valuable tool here.

A central part of the design work focuses on the database and applications. To the extent that the analysis has been well executed, this major task will be made easier. To begin it, decisions must be made on how to implement entities, especially super- and subtypes, as tables. There may also be a need for some denormalization to improve performance on frequently requested data. Performance that is not designed into a system is later achieved only at a much higher cost. Then default table and column definitions are generated. These are refined, validation and derivation expressions are added, and indexes are defined. All these actions are executed and stored using CASE*Dictionary.

A utility is available that creates a "first cut" of module definitions. Module types defined are screens, reports, utilities (often batch programs) and manual procedures. The consultants begin refining data usages of these modules and add module-specific validation and derivation expressions to them. Needless to say, much detailed work goes into the design of screens, reports, and utilities. After these first-cut definitions have been tailored, a similar utility can be run that generates a first cut of the menu hierarchy, which can also be refined.

By the end of this stage, feasible and well-documented designs both of the database and application modules should be ready for implementation. Where required, the network architecture design should also be complete. The consultants also need to think in more detail about other issues: user training, delivery and acceptance, data conversion, and manual processes. In other words, they need to begin designing the transition stage. For example, defining the availability of the application (hours of the day, excluding maintenance time) helps to set user expectations correctly. Another deliverable provides details of how the design fulfills security and administrative functions.

Build

With definitions stored in CASE*Dictionary, the task of implementing them is fairly straight-forward. A utility creates scripts for the definition of the database, tablespace, tables, views, indexes, constraints, and even ORACLE users. These scripts are fully portable to other ORACLE platforms. Without any changes they can be run wherever and whenever they are needed—first, of course, in the test environment. At this point sufficient meaningful test data should be entered, not only for program tests, but also for performance tuning.

To create the required modules, user preferences and table and column usages are first manipu-lated, then the CASE generators are employed to produce an application with zero-defect code. In order to implement all of the required functionality, however, that generated code might need to be enhanced. Generating an application module is a frequently repeated process in any Oracle CASE project, especially at the beginning of this stage when user preference settings and templates are still being manipulated to establish look-and-feel conventions. But once those basic decisions have been made, developers can concentrate on creating an efficient and functional application. In fact, because the agreed-upon conventions are stored in CASE*Dictionary, they can be enforced for any subsequent work done on that application.

The build stage is concerned not only with producing an application but with thorough testing as well. Bottom-up unit tests for functionality and exceptions are followed by link and system tests for integration and performance. The documentation of test results makes error repair more efficient and reduces the number of test iterations. It also provides detailed technical information for change requests, which are especially useful if users are involved in the system test (an involvement we recommend).

User Documentation

The user documentation stage occurs simultanously with the build stage. Documentation (including training material) for users and technical staff needs to be provided appropriately and effectively and must also be finished in time for acceptance testing. Working from the same CASE*Dictionary specifications as the software developers, technical writers have enough time to do a high-quality job. Another "miracle" of CASE is that a lot of system documentation is built in. CASE*Dictionary users can choose from an ever-increasing number of existing reports (including impact analysis reports) or create their own based on information stored in the repository.

Transition

The skill most needed for a smooth transition into a production environment is the ability to coordinate many different tasks: to work with dependencies, deadlines, and availability of all the necessary parties involved. For many computer professionals this is the time of nightmares, but it doesn't have to be that way. The necessary tasks of the transition were recorded during analysis, details and dependencies were added during design, plans were reviewed during the build stage, so now those plans are being executed. Usually the hardware installation is done first, followed by the software installation, which consists of scripts generated by a CASE*Dictionary utility (the DDL Generator) and menus, forms, and reports created by Oracle's CASE generators. The next step is data conversion. Then, with the real data in place, the application's co-existence with other systems can be tested along with the operating conditions of any distributed processes or databases. After establishing support and training the users, final acceptance testing can be performed. Throughout this process the transition plan is followed and a detailed fault log is kept to avoid unnecessary repetitions of error checking. The aim is to install the new system with minimal interruptions of the business.

Production

During the production stage we aim at a reliable, smoothly running system maintained at a high service level. Regular operational duties such as backing up, archiving, auditing, and gathering performance statistics support the first part of this goal. The second part requires a timely response to user requests, and this depends on effective impact analysis for which the CASE tools provide reports and matrices. When the decision has been made to carry out a particular enhancement, CASE*Dictionary definitions must first be changed. On that basis, amended programs are generated. Of course, this approach would not be suitable in an emergency, in which case the problem would simply be fixed as quickly as possible. For any alterations outside of CASE, the reverse engineering facilities are used to keep the definitions in CASE*Dictionary in synch with the current database and applications. Otherwise the consultants lose what they have worked so hard to achieve: a completely documented, truly manageable system.

1.3 Workshop Timeline

The following is an approximate timeline for an ideally conducted ten-day CASE workshop. Variations, of course, can result from the wishes of clients as well as from a wide range of other project-specific circumstances.

Before:

- Agreement upon a suitable functional area as scope for the workshop
- Acquisition of background documentation
- Selection of participants
- Scheduling of key interviews

Day 1:

- Introduction to the team
- Overview of CASE*Method, aims, techniques, and tools
- Preparation for interviews
- Directional interviews
- Information modeling: introduction to function and entity modeling

Day 2:

- Setting up an application
- Introduction to using CASE*Designer and CASE*Dictionary
- Generating strategy-level reports
- Carrying out feedback sessions
- Consolidating the results of feedback sessions
- Discussion on doing a strategy report for management

Day 3:

- Preparing for analysis-level interviews

- Interviewing for business details
- Advanced modeling techniques
- Normalization
- Defining attributes, domains, and unique identifiers

Day 4:

- Refining models, iteration of interviews
- Reaching the detailed level: elementary functions
- Discussion on achieving an essential ERD
- Dataflow diagrams
- Cross-checking models

Day 5:

- Considering distributed requirements
- Planning the transition to a "live" system
- Generating analysis-level reports
- Preparing and holding the final feedback session
- Consolidating the results of the final feedback session

Day 6:

- Turning entities into tables
- Default database design
- Refining the design: creating sequences, validating columns
- Using Edit Text

Day 7:

- Referential integrity
- Defining indexes
- Creating the database and its objects
- Implementing reference tables

Day 8:

- Using the Default Application Design Utility
- Accepting and refining module definitions
- Data usage of modules
- CASE*Generator for SQL*Forms

Day 9:

- User preferences
- Refining SQL*Forms applications
- Generating reports in SQL*Plus and SQL*ReportWriter
- Refining the reports

Day 10:

- CASE*Generator for SQL*Menu
- Integration test
- Outstanding questions and issues

The following topics are often added here, if desired:

- Impact analysis
- Overview of CASE administration

2

Planning

No CASE study is complete without an attempt to understand the organization's strategic objectives and direction. Only when armed with such information can an analyst develop systems that truly respond to mission-critical requirements. In this chapter we approach the strategy stage of a business system life cycle from different points of view. On the one hand we introduce the major topics that would be included in a fully executed enterprise-wide strategy study. We also show how some of these subjects, such as interviewing senior management for business direction, can be included within the limited frame of a CASE workshop. But in doing so, we examine the ways in which the larger organization's objectives influence the functional area being studied in our workshop (which can be called *project strategy*). Then we show how to model the information we've gained by using CASE*Dictionary and CASE*Designer.

2.1   A CASE Study Scenario

We're a small consulting firm that has been approached by the IS manager of a business that we'll call Karl's Vineyard and Winery (KVW). He tells us that he wants to build an enterprise-wide information system using their recently acquired ORACLE RDBMS and development tools. His decision to go with Oracle in the first place has come largely from a desire to utilize an integrated CASE (I-CASE) tools set, including repository-based code generators for all aspects of application development (CASE generators). The winery is at an early stage of growth and its organization is going through rapid changes, so he feels that a completely documented business model in CASE*Dictionary will provide the best means for monitoring new developments and providing applications to meet them quickly, accurately, and reliably.

By the time we arrive on the scene, KVW has been cultivating grapevines for a decade, but selling wine for only three years. They've entered the market at a difficult time and, although sales have been increasing steadily, the international wine industry is still in a substantial recession. Consequently, the company's decision makers are reluctant to allocate the funds necessary for a full-scale CASE project.

2.2   The Workshop Method

In a situation like this, we've found that a workshop approach to introducing CASE tools is most effective. To set this up, we first meet with the sponsoring user and establish the scope of a small CASE project that can be accomplished in approximately ten days. We use this time frame because we want to provide a quick "proof" of CASE at a reduced cost. The project is a workshop because members of our client's IS staff are involved in the whole process, from strategy to database and application generation. Our sponsoring user identifies four to six participants who will be most likely to use CASE in the future, and we all work together as a team. So the workshop is intended to 1) prove the value of CASE by delivering a high-quality database and application in a very short time and 2) serve as the medium for a technology transfer that will provide participants with a solid introduction to CASE tools and their underlying techniques.

Still, we'd ultimately like our clients to apply CASE methods on an enterprise-wide scale where they can do the most good. So we make every effort to ensure that after the workshop our sponsor can return to senior management with solid benefits on which to base his or her request for a strategy study of the entire organization. By developing complete business models and storing them in CASE*Dictionary, newly-trained staff will be able to design and implement management controls on future application development, helping to ensure that those systems are not only highly functional and fully integrated with one another, but also that they focus on the business's primary objectives (which can also be amended in CASE*Dictionary at any time). Additionally, they will be able to build any subsequent applications using the same automated methods employed in our workshop.

It's not always possible to obtain total management commitment to CASE after just one workshop. The project's results, suitably packaged and presented, can help decision makers see the value of using CASE to coordinate IS development for the entire organization. But if they're still reluctant, the sponsoring user can conduct a pilot project, with a larger scope than the workshop, that, when successfully concluded, will provide a stronger "proof of concept." Ideally, however, a complete strategy study should be accomplished as early in the process as possible. This way, "top-down" controlling mechanisms such as critical success factors, key performance indicators, and business constraints can guide IS development, eliminating misunderstood priorities and other expensive, unnecessary errors.

2.3 Preparing for Our Workshop

In speaking to our sponsoring user (the IS manager), we find that his staff is small, which means that we can only expect to get a few people involved in the workshop. But by the project's end, they'll be in a position to deliver many benefits, especially to a medium-sized organization like KVW. Fortunately, all of them have a working knowledge of SQL*Plus and SQL*Forms, because these are really prerequisites for a successful workshop. Learning the basics of SQL and how to navigate through SQL*Forms requires some "digestion" time. These are subjects for workshops in their own right and should not be combined with a tight schedule of training in the more sophisticated CASE tools.

A rule of thumb we use in calculating the right scope for this kind of project is to encompass as many entities as there are working days in a workshop. We've agreed upon a challenging but reasonably small scope for our project. We'll be working primarily with the sales administration of the winery, an area that the IS manager considers critical. He explains that KVW has already invested heavily in the organization of their vineyard and winery, accomplishing the difficult task of producing world-class wines from a rather large vineyard. But due to the recession, these award-winning bottles are accumulating in storage and the sales sector has become a major priority. Additionally, sales administration, unlike vineyard management or wine production, is of a workable scope considering our time constraints. To give an overview of the business and a picture of how the "Manage sales . . ." function fits into it, we've provided an enterprise-wide top-level function hierarchy that our client was later able to model after full funding for a CASE study was obtained (see Appendix D).

2.4 An Introduction to the Team

We begin the workshop by holding an introductory meeting with the new team. Our sponsoring user has already spoken individually with each prospective team member and has assured us that we'll get their full cooperation. We begin by having everyone introduce themselves and briefly describe their backgrounds, current responsibilities, and knowledge of CASE methods and Oracle tools. We get a variety of responses that give us an idea where to begin our introduction of the workshop. We emphasize (as we continue to do in this book) how and where the various activities of the workshop belong in relation to the business systems life cycle and to the CASE method. In short, we try to provide an overview of our aims and techniques. Then we throw the meeting open for questions, partly to help clarify the subject and, of course, partly so that we can start getting acquainted. A CASE workshop is an intense experience and it's essential to establish a positive and supportive atmosphere within the team as soon as possible.

2.5   Interviewing for Business "Direction" and Boundaries

In the workshop we target a small subset of the business, but to do so effectively we still need to form a top-down view of KVW that includes the company's major objectives, directions, and priorities. An efficient way to do this is to conduct directional interviews (no longer than an hour each) with the primary decision makers in the company. Additionally, we collect and read any available written material on the company and its goals.

On Boxes and Strategies

Throughout the text, you'll see boxes such as this with text visually separated from the rest of the material. This distinguishes two types of information that we consider supplementary, like footnotes. The first type includes subjects that are beyond the scope of our sample workshop project. The other type contains technical details that, because they seem particularly useful or difficult to find elsewhere, we've included in greater depth than in our other technical descriptions. Our first box subject is strategies.

As alluded to in the introduction to this chapter, the term *strategy* can refer either to a study of an entire organization or to the interfaces between the enterprise as a whole and the particular functional area being examined. Both definitions of strategy are valid and useful, but we also need to distinguish between them. Whenever a subject is more closely related to an enterprise-wide strategy stage, we try to point this out. And clearly, no workshop can arrive at anything approaching a complete organizational model (nor can most smaller CASE projects). But we can strive for as thorough an understanding as possible of the impact of the larger organization on our area of study and analysis.

One purpose for conducting directional interviews, in the context of a complete strategy stage, is to compile a list of perceived functional areas and the people most knowledgeable about them. If we were now able to carry out an enterprise-wide study, this data would provide the basis for another set of more detailed interviews at the analysis level. Where necessary, we would break out (or "decompose") these functions into a more detailed level of the business's function hierarchy, as seen in the top-level model above (see Appendix D). Each functional area, together with its subordinate functions, also provides an appropriate scale for the design of a detailed entity-relationship diagram (ERD) and one or more dataflow diagrams (DFD).

In accordance with the scope of our workshop, we need to decompose the intermediate function "Manage wine sales..." (SALES_1, see Appendix D) into its subordinate functions, and for that purpose we interview the sales administration manager after the directional interviews are done. We also develop an ERD model for SALES_1 (see Fig. 2.6) and a context diagram (high-level DFD, see Fig. 3.10) to show the interfaces to other systems.

In the time frame of a small workshop, however, it's often impossible to schedule directional interviews. When this happens we need to look elsewhere for our high-level information. Three useful sources are

1. the company's official mission statement (often available in writing),

2. annual reports, and

3. organizational charts.

"Org" charts shouldn't be confused with function hierarchies, but they can provide a valuable overview of how management perceives the division of business sectors.

2.6   On Introductory Briefings

In a fully executed strategy stage, depending on the size of the organization being studied, some sort of general briefing session for all prospective interviewees can provide an excellent introduction and help smooth over any initial anxiety or reservations held toward our information-gathering process. We recommend that all interviewees attend this meeting, not only because it allows us to explain our aims and methods to everyone at once, but also because the participants will realize that all their peers and, perhaps, superiors are involved in the process with them. This usually engenders a more receptive attitude toward the study and its techniques.

The briefing should be true to its name (brief) and yet communicate the potential benefits of thoroughly examining the business. We try to concentrate, at this high-level stage, on direct benefits to the company rather than on specific IS topics. For example, we might point out that by identifying primary business objectives, priorities, and business constraints as well as key performance indicators and critical success factors, the study not only articulates these elements for the entire organization, but actually stores them in a central repository (see Fig. 2.1) where they can be used as a guide to ensure that all future IS development concentrates on mission-critical applications. We also stress that any directional changes can immediately be reflected in this business model simply by reiterating the study process.

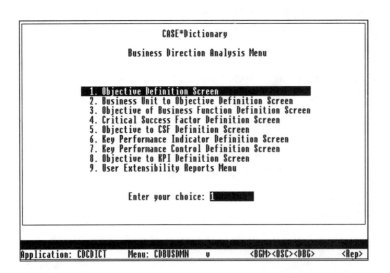

Figure 2.1
Business Direction
Analysis Menu

In our workshop, especially because of the organization's smaller scale but also due to time constraints, we've chosen to explain ourselves individually, in a more relaxed and conversational environment, to the few people we'll be interviewing at this stage.

2.7   On Interviewing

Interviewing is probably the most important single skill used in a strategy study, and it is critical to the success of our workshop. The ability to ask the most clearly phrased, most appropriate questions is especially important when we're dealing with people, like senior management, whose time is very limited and who are often unacquainted with most of an IS specialist's daily vocabulary.

We've found it best if an interview can be conducted by two analysts, one who asks the questions and the other who records and organizes notes. Although the interviewer's role is more visible, the note taker's is just as important, since it involves summarizing and clarifying a mass of information. If possible, it's also useful for the interviewer to take notes for later comparison. Sometimes we tape interviews, especially if only one of us can be present. However, a tape recorder can evoke discomfort in some people, and we try to be sure that such a reaction won't be forthcoming before we use it.

To introduce our new team members to the interviewing process we employ a couple of methods. One is to organize "test-run" interviews, where our participants question one of us or, perhaps, the sponsoring user. This is a very effective tool that is worth trying to fit into a tight schedule. Another method is to have them play the role of note takers at actual interviews (after some introductory training on methods). Once they've "gotten their feet wet" they feel more confident to do the interviewing themselves.

Ideally we want all participants in our workshop to act both as interviewers and note takers, but in practice we often focus on teaching interviewing to those with the most communications skills. Others might be more suited to note taking. The aim is to leave our client by the end of the workshop with at least one good interviewing team that can do any additional training themselves. This is the essence of a "tech-transfer."

Selecting interviewees is an ongoing process whereby we begin with the highest-level decision makers available, then use our notes and recommendations from the interviewees to choose the next round of subjects. We also take recommendations from our sponsoring user, while being careful not to limit ourselves to a pre-set list. Sometimes the real opinion leaders or most influential people in a business area are not necessarily the managers. We need to interview these people, too, if our project is to be effective and well received. As we progress through the analysis stage, we may uncover a wider range of people to talk with. We might also discover the need for additional meetings with previous interviewees, perhaps on a more detailed level. At the same time, we need to keep the scope of our workshop project clearly in mind. It's all too easy to become overly ambitious when applying powerful analysis tools within a constricted time frame.

2.8   How to Begin?

For many people, knowing how to begin an interview is a major task. Our experience has revealed a few pointers:

- Try to arrive at the meeting already prepared with notes about the person's responsibilites and background, and be clear about your objectives for holding this interview.

- Be prepared with a list of keywords. These are terms either that are common to the industry or business unit type that you're addressing or that you've encountered in previous meetings or briefings in the company (see Fig. 2.2).

- Be ready to spend some time, besides with the usual (and quite necessary) pleasantries, familiarizing the person with your objectives and, if required, selling CASE methods.

- Emphasize the need to avoid interruptions. Much valuable time and energy can be lost when a discussion is broken off just as a complex subject was on the verge of being successfully explored.

- Remind your interviewee that your conversation will remain confidential and that the results will be in the form of diagrams rather than "minutes."

- Continue with a specific briefing that will vary according to the scale of the interview. For example, on a detailed level, concentrate on clarifying the scope of questioning and verifying the person's area of responsibility and competence.

- Point out that in subsequent feedback sessions there will be ample opportunity to review your models until everyone is satisfied with their completeness and accuracy.

- Use the language of your interviewees. Keep track of the business terminology and ask when unfamiliar jargon or acronyms are used.

We have now laid the groundwork for our interview. It's useful to have a prepared first question included in our notes, though we should not rely on it. Often the interaction that has resulted from our little briefing will stimulate a more appropriate lead-in to the interview. One basic rule is to try to begin with an open question from the top, that is, formulated in the most general or inclusive manner that is suitable to the scope of the interview. For example, a vice president might be asked: "What are the key objectives of your organization?" or, perhaps, "What are the most critical factors for the success of your company?" A department head could be approached with: "What do you see as the primary roles and responsibilities of your group?" Now we have established the "top of the pyramid" and can proceed to include more structure and detail based on these primary objectives.

```
INTERVIEW
Name: Tom Jones
Position: Sales Admin Mgr                    Interviewer:  Jeff
Date/Time:  Sept 6, '92  2 p.m.              Notetaker:    Mary
Location:  KVW Conference Room


INTRODUCTION:
Pleasantries, briefing, confidentiality


INITIAL QUESTIONS:
• What are the objectives of your group?
• Tell us about your responsibilities as sales administrator.
• What has to be done to administer Sales most efficiently?
• How do you measure your success?
• What's your most serious problem?
• What kinds of information do you need the most?


KEYWORDS:
customer
customer problems
delivery
invoice
line item
order
price, pricing system
wine


SUMMARY:
We've talked about ....
Let's go through it again quickly and see whether we've
covered everything.


GENERAL CONCLUSION:
Ensure he feels that he's made a contribution.
Contact us if you think of anything else.
Feedback is ....
```

Figure 2.2

Preparation for Interviews

2.9   Our Directional Interviews

Before even arriving at KVW we arranged interviews with its vice president and its international sales director, knowing that it would be difficult to do this on short notice. We begin our meeting with the VP by complimenting him on the beautiful setting of his mountain vineyard, then we chat briefly about wine. After a couple of minutes we begin explaining our aims for the interview, including all the points mentioned above. When we ask him about the objectives of KVW, his first words are very helpful: *"We're involved in trying to establish a premium wine brand.*" This is already close to a mission statement for KVW, and it focuses our picture of this company considerably in relation to the wine-producing industry as a whole. Here are some other quotations from the interview:

> I'd say a five-year aim has been to establish KVW at least in the consciousness of connoiseurs of wine and the trade as a premium producer. And we've been willing to sacrifice immediate sales in order to keep from discounting excessively. So the nice thing about that is we've been able to do this and to achieve a decent sales level in a really competitive discounting environment, which this industry is right now.

> So what we're trying to do in the next couple of years is continue establishing the distribution system which, in the U.S., would mean a distributor in each major market. In foreign markets it would mean an importer for each market. Along with this we're continuing to set up the foundations of a positive relationship with the trade, with restaurants and bottle shops, etc., and be in a position when we emerge as a major name—whether through favorable press, reviews of our wines, or through a more substantial advertising budget of our own—when any or all of this happens, which I'm sure it will, to have the mechanisms in place to deliver any quantities of wine to the consumer.

From these comments and others in this half-hour interview, we arrive at the following formulation, which the vice president later acknowledged to be a suitable mission statement. It could serve as the top function in an enterprise-wide function hierarchy (see Appendix D): "Produce the finest wines possible and provide them efficiently to the customer with the least possible discounting of prices."

Similarly, we're able to extract the following three critical success factors:

1. production of premium-quality wines,

2. efficient, large-scale distribution network, and

3. competitive pricing that avoids discounting.

We then interview the international sales director. We've learned that he was responsible for setting up the original sales organization. Knowing this makes it easier for us to focus on specific questions. Since his schedule involves a lot of travel and we aren't sure if we can arrange a second interview, we try to gather information both on a directional level and more specifically on the sales organization's structure and administration.

Here are some of the interview's main points:

> If you have limited production, then the aim of the company is first, to produce that most efficiently, that is, using fewer and fewer resources, and second, to achieve the highest possible price for it.

> You have to analyze what markets are better to be in. How much money do you have to spend to service your local customers or your domestic distributors or your importers? Again, you only have a limited amount of your product, so the more information you have about detailed expenditures in relation to sales in a given market, the better.

> The aim of the company has to be to make the best of our limited amount of goods in two ways. One is leading up to the moment when a bottle of wine is ready and the other is leading away from it.

> I would like to have on my desk, every day, three things: what do we have in stock, who bought something yesterday, and how much money people owe us. From there you develop your plan. You know where to put your energy. But it's a problem getting these data because they come from different sources. The inventory comes from the production department. Then sales and shipping have to interact with production on the orders, and finally the sales information has to go to accounts receivable. We also have to be current enough to know what orders are pending so we don't commit inventory that may already be sold. We've just installed a network between production and shipping, but down at the sales office we aren't current. It's very embarrassing when you call an important customer and you don't know he's just ordered.

We're able to gather quite a bit of detailed information in this interview, much of it, as planned, referring more to the analysis stage than to strategy. From the quotations listed above we note some interesting points. One obviously recurring theme is the idea of limited production. Here's a business that harvests a fixed amount of "raw material" once a year (grapes), then spends the rest of its production time dealing with it in a strictly prescribed manner. This means, for instance, that faster processing of products is only desirable after the wine is ready to package. Until then, efficiency has to be measured quite differently, perhaps by use of resources. Again, if we were conducting a complete strategy study at this point such information would help us form our model of the production system for further analysis. In this case, all we can now do is to take detailed notes, model them roughly, and pass these on to our sponsoring user for a later, more extensive project.

Another point regards the lack of data integration. Isolated applications and files especially prevent the sales administration from performing properly. We'll need to keep these interfaces in mind as we design our system and we'll start by including them in our context dataflow diagram (see Fig. 3.10). Third, the sales director has focused on a need to analyze expenses versus sales in specific markets. Since this involves extensive access to current financial information, it is outside the scope of our project. It can, however, be noted for inclusion in the complete business model that, we hope, will later be funded.

We are also able to identify some of the functions and entities that should be included in the scope of our workshop. These can be seen in Figures 2.5 and 2.6. The shipping department is located in the winery's main warehouse where the packaged, tax-paid wine is initially stored. As a result of this physical proximity, it was originally considered part of the production functional area. But, as the sales director puts it,

> In any organization there's a conflict between production and service-oriented groups because production, by its nature, is highly structured and tends to be inflexible while sales, for example, has to respond quickly to unexpected customer requests.

Now the sales administration and shipping department are very closely linked, which also makes sense from the sales director's point of view—that the flow of activity "leading away" from a finished bottle of wine all belongs to the same process. We'll try to include as many shipping functions as possible in our project.

Additionally, we've confirmed that all promotional activities leading up to a sale belong to the marketing sector, and that the sales administration is responsible only for handling whatever occurs after a customer places an order. All this information lays the groundwork for another round of interviews with the people responsible for these subordinate functions.

It is useful here to make one initial comment about defining entities. During strategy, when modeling is done on a high level with little detail, analysts often tend to work without formally defining any attributes or adding description text to entity definitions. Our experience is that such omissions can cause problems. Often there will be two or more conflicting but unarticulated definitions of an entity held within a development team. By defining one or two attributes for each entity and adding a description, we begin to discover these discrepancies of understanding and to reach a consensus on entity definitions. This is especially important at this early stage because subsequent detailed modeling will be done on the basis of this high-level data structure.

2.10   Recording Strategy-level Information

With so much information suddenly available, we need to begin recording it right away in CASE*Designer. Having just come out of those interviews, the understanding we have gained is still easily discernible through our notes. But the longer we wait to fix that new knowledge in the form of models, the more likely we will be to find ourselves with a pile of undecipherable markings.

CASE*Designer provides a graphical user interface (GUI) for designing models and creating cross-checking matrices. It simultaneously stores the underlying information in CASE*Dictionary tables. It also functions as an integrated, multi-windowed hub for directly accessing CASE*Dictionary and the CASE generators, as well as SQL*Plus, SQL*Forms, and SQL*ReportWriter. During our strategy stage we primarily need to use two tools in CASE*Designer: the Function Hierarchy Diagrammer and the Entity Relationship Diagrammer. The first of these allows us to model the business's data requirements; the other provides a graphical workspace for creating a hierarchy of its processes or functions. The use of these techniques together is essential to our understanding of an organization's information needs.

2.11   Access to CASE

For the installation or upgrade of the CASE Tools version 5.0, two ORACLE users are required: SYSTEM (or a DBA account) and SYSCASE, which is the owner of the CASE definition tables. In other words, the userid SYSCASE owns the structure of the CASE tables but not the user-specific data.

The CASE tables themselves, which hold information on such things as applications, functions, and entities, are owned by another user (one per CASE instance). We could call it a CASE Administrator or CASE Owner. This user requires CONNECT and RESOURCE privileges and the CMAN role in SQL*Menu.

Software developers (CASE users) need to have at least the CONNECT privilege (although they often have the RESOURCE privilege) and the CDICT role that is assigned in SQL*Menu. A CASE Administrator or Owner needs to GRANT full or read-only access to every CASE user because he or she will use the CASE tables via synonyms that a script sets up upon the first log-on. From then on the CASE user may use CASE as if it were his or her own repository (besides some DBA functions).

There's also a one-of-a-kind read-only CASE user, the "User Defined Reporter," who can create customized reports based on views to CASE*Dictionary tables. Whoever knows the password of this userid may access the User Defined Reporting views. This special userid exists only once per repository.

2.12   Initial Set-up of an Application

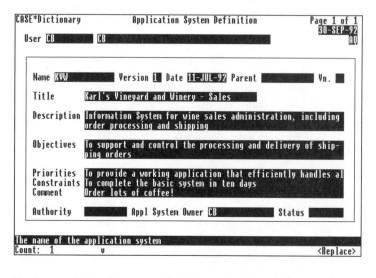

Figure 2.3
Application System
Definition Screen

Having established access to CASE, our CASE Administrator sets up our application as shown in Figure 2.3. Consistent with CASE*Method, space is provided in CASE*Dictionary for defining our own objectives, priorities, and any constraints placed on our project.

Next we declare our new application to be our "User Preference." To do this, we have to use any screen that begins with the field "Appl". After moving our cursor to "Appl", we press the [User Preferences] key to open a pop-up window that allows us to enter and commit our application name. (See Fig. 2.4 where, although it doesn't show up on our screen shot, we also define a business unit called SALES.) From now on "KVW" will be our default application name whenever we enter a screen, run a utility, or draw a diagram. Even while stopping and starting the ORACLE database our default won't get lost.

Figure 2.4
Business Unit Definition
Screen—Preferred
Application

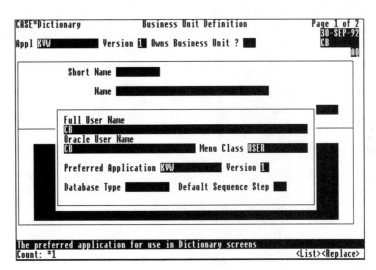

2.13   Diagramming Functions in CASE*Designer

Now it's time to exit CASE*Dictionary and enter CASE*Designer. Once an application has been specified, the so-called flying grid main menu screen of CASE*Designer appears. This is that central hub from which a variety of Oracle tools can be accessed. Using the "Techniques" pull-down menu, we select the "Function Diagrammer" and enter our functions directly into "soft boxes" on its graphical workspace (see Fig. 2.5). We also need to define function labels. CASE*Method recommends a hierarchical scheme, which we have followed on the top and intermediate levels. But our client has requested that we use their naming conventions for the lower-level functions. When we create new functions with labels and definitions here, the underlying CASE*Dictionary tables are automatically updated.

Only one function hierarchy can be held per application version. This forces us to consolidate the understandings of all our team members (and on larger projects, of all teams), so that we arrive at one common process model of the business that is valid at one point in time.

We could have created our function hierarchy without loading CASE*Designer by working directly from CASE*Dictionary, using the *Function Hierarchy Screen* under the *Strategy Menu.* We choose to use CASE*Designer because it provides excellent integration and the convenience of a GUI. From within the diagrammers we can directly access related CASE*Dictionary screens as windows.

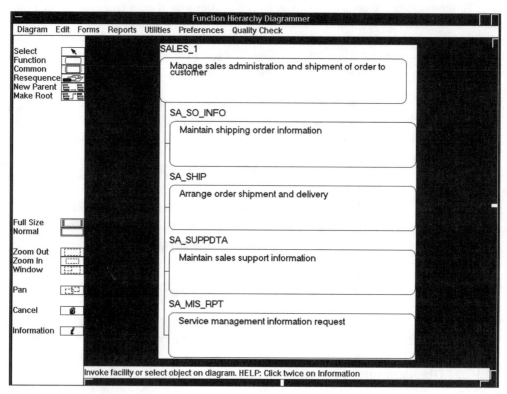

Figure 2.5 Function Hierarchy Diagrammer

2.14   Using the Entity Relationship Diagrammer

Having established the top levels of our function hierarchy, we are ready to employ the Entity Relationship Diagrammer. This tool's GUI is a workspace where we can design entity relationship diagrams: models of an organization's data structure that include entities, attributes, and relationships between entities (see Section 5.13 for some excellent reference material on ERDs). Besides aiding our understanding of business systems, these images can reveal flaws in data analysis and even in existing business practices and IS applications. Our first task in using this technique is to draw those entities and relationships that correspond to the functions we've so far uncovered in our interviews.

Even before exploring the ER Diagrammer, our team members spend some time building hand-drawn top-level ERDs based on interview notes. Although we know our picture of the "SALES" business unit is still rather sketchy, it is important for all participants to begin designing ERDs, both in order to learn the techniques involved and to increase their understanding of the information we've collected so far.

Because the Entity Relationship Diagrammer is fundamentally a more graphical device than the Function Hierarchy Diagrammer, its GUI is a bit more complex and needs more time to master. For example, there are many diagram-size options to choose from, and we need to select one before we can even define an entity on our first model.

An analyst experienced on CASE*Designer can actually use the ER Diagrammer for brainstorming, as if sketching on a notepad, but it's good to be aware that entities and relationships immediately get stored in CASE*Dictionary and that such "scribbling" has an impact on all other users of the application.

We don't provide here a tutorial on the ER Diagrammer: this has been satisfactorily done elsewhere (e.g., in Oracle manuals). But we can offer a few pointers to help overcome some technical obstacles and hasten mastery of the technique.

- Hold to some basic form rules when laying out your ERD:

  1) Don't crowd your diagram. This is why all those different diagram sizes are available. An ERD is a communication tool, not a showcase for displaying intimidating masterpieces of abstract genius.

  2) "Crows fly south and east"—that is, have the "Many" end of each relationship (called a "crow's foot") point its claws upward or to the left of your diagram. This concentrates high-volume entities (those with many occurences) in the top left area of the ERD. The eye can then follow their relationships toward the low-volume entities in the opposite corner, providing the model with a clear and logical structure.

  3) Try to minimize relationship lines crossing one another and try to avoid angled lines. This will help create a clean, readable impression.

  4) Vary the sizes of your entity boxes (avoiding angled relationship lines will cause this to happen anyway)—they make the diagram more distinctive and interesting. Appropriately, more important entities will generally appear larger to handle a greater number of relationships. You'll be showing your model to people who aren't used to reading ERDs, and it helps them be able visually to distinguish one diagram from another.

- When naming entities, be sure to use the singular form:

  1) they correspond to the correct syntax for reading the ERD, and

  2) default table names are built from the generated plurals.

- Also be sure the entity name is *really* singular: "Personnel," "Equipment," "Inventory," and anything ending in "List" are really plurals because they refer to collections of things.

- Don't hesitate to build ERDs for your feedback sessions that are subsets or combinations of existing ones. Modeling only the entities and relationships that directly concern your interviewees not only aids their understanding but also gives you a fresh perspective on the whole that may reveal important new information.

- Carefully consider your relationship descriptions. We've noticed a tendency to make them either too simple or too complex. They best ones are truly descriptive *and* concise.

- Use the "Window" button so that you can focus on exactly the scale of the diagram you want to work with. The "Zoom-In" and "Zoom-Out" buttons don't provide as fine a scale gradation. Additionally, zooming in doesn't allow you to specify the location of the new image, so you usually have to scroll vertically and/or horizontally even if the image size happens to be right.

- Regularly use the "Consolidate Entity" and "Consolidate Relationship" options on the Edit Menu to ensure that any changes saved into CASE*Dictionary by other users of the application can be incorporated into your ERD (and even if you don't want them on your diagram, you'll surely want to be aware of them).

- A one-to-many relationship with an optional dashed line on the crow's-foot end is very difficult to read when the scale is fairly small (maybe this is punishment for defining a somewhat uncommon relationship).

- Don't connect the "many" end of a relationship to the corner of an entity box—it will appear as a single line.

- When you delete all but one entity that was part of an arc relationship in CASE*Designer, that remaining entity will remain tagged as forming part of an arc until you change it in the Relationship Definition screen in CASE*Dictionary (remove the "1" in the "Arc" field).

2.15   Strategy Summary

In a full-scale strategy study, now would be the time to deliver a report with recommendations to senior management such as we described in our introduction. In our workshop, however, we end Day Two with a discussion on how such report presentations can be handled. This includes an introduction on the screens and reports associated with the *Business Directions Analysis Menu* (see Fig. 2.1). These allow the documenting and linking to one another of business objectives, critical success factors, and key performance indicators as well as other elements deemed valuable by an organization and defined under "User Extensibility" (see Appendix A).

At this stage our ERD and function hierarchy are still fairly basic (see Figs. 2.5 and 2.6). For the time being, uncomplicated models are the most suitable for presenting to decision makers at any feedback sessions. They provide an adequate high-level business model without too many details obscuring its basic structure. But in the analysis stage it is exactly those details, inappropriate now, that will provide the backbone for a high-quality database and application design.

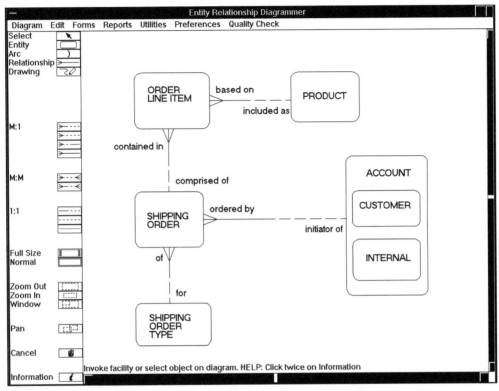

Figure 2.6 Entity Relationship Diagrammer

3

Analysis

During the analysis stage, specifications for a business system based on one functional area of an organization must be fully detailed (and, of course, understood), then stored in CASE*Dictionary along with clear, accurate, and complete models of both data and processes. This information will provide the foundation for a high-quality database and application design.

3.1   Preparing for a Detailed Look at the Business

We've now completed the second day of our workshop. Together with our team members we've been studying interview tapes and poring over and discussing our notes as we refine the high-level models.

Whereas the strategy stage in a full-scale CASE project is intended to provide an enterprise-wide view of the business in the form of high-level functions and entities as well as objectives, directions, and business constraints, analysis focuses on detailed information requirements. Time and scope constraints have forced us, for the most part, to limit our strategy study to the enterprise's impact on the functional area being handled by our workshop. But now we have the chance to carry out a fairly thorough systems analysis within that scope. However, this is no small task. During this stage, we want to:

- produce accurate and detailed models through reiterated interviewing, analysis, and feedback;

- estimate entity volumes and function frequencies;

- thoroughly cross-check models by employing matrix techniques and determine key element associations and usages; and

- ascertain any distributed requirements as well as any known design constraints.

3.2   An Analysis Interview

We begin our next level of interviewing by targeting the SALES_1 function and its subordinate functions. We start at the highest level appropriate to this functional area by meeting with the sales administration manager. According to information we gained from the international sales director, this manager is involved with all the functions except SA_SHIP (see Fig. 2.5) on the function hierarchy that we modeled from that last interview. One of our primary objectives now will be to uncover more functions at this level.

During a full-scale CASE project, analysis interviews can often last about half a day. In a workshop, however, we try to work in segments of approximately one hour to keep the subsequent modeling manageable for our participants.

When we ask our interviewee about the objectives of his group, he describes them this way:

> We need to organize the flow and storage of sales-related information, especially what relates to shipping orders, so we create and maintain systems to keep that information accurate and accessible. We're also responsible for helping to maintain relationships with our customers by communicating with them about sales and products.

He tells us that his most critical data are held on customers and shipping orders. He also gives us some completely new information by explaining that his department has taken over accounts receivable (A/R) from the accounting department. Here's what he says:

Normally A/R is handled by accounting but in our case there's a federal law that prohibits us from selling wine to any wholesale customer who's over 42 days late on a payment, unless it goes COD. Since accounting is located across town and was understaffed at the time, we decided to take over A/R so that we'd know the current status of our customers when their orders came in.

One immediate observation we make about this circumstance is that if accounting could provide accurate, on-line A/R information, the sales administration wouldn't need to carry this task, which would release staff for functions more intrinsically related to its objectives. The same could probably be said of invoicing and crediting customers, which are tasks related to A/R also being handled by the sales administration. Since the time constraints of our workshop won't allow us to construct an A/R function under SALES_1, we decide to limit our scope to functions and entities more essentially related to sales administration. The only A/R-related function we'll include is "Invoice customer for shipping order", where we simply initiate the billing process, then pass it on to A/R.

Another function we need to add under SALES_1 is "Track status of shipping order". The shipping department, besides delivering the wine themselves, also send orders to delivery services to ship from external warehouses. The status of those deliveries is critical from a customer-service point of view as well as for A/R, who need signed delivery receipts in event of any financial dispute.

More information about entities begins to emerge. During our last interview we found that accounts needed to be fundamentally divided into entity subtypes: "Customers" and "Internal" (internal accounts charged to cost centers). We now discover that customers should be further subdivided between "Special" clients who are invoiced for their purchases and "Retail" customers, about whom much less information is needed and whose shipping orders are processed quite differently: they must pay in advance for wine. We're also able to isolate some reference entities containing "type" information (for example, about accounts and shipping orders as in Fig. 3.1). Account types are particularly important to distinguish different classes of special customers (e.g., Distributors, Restaurants, Bottle Shops, etc.). And to cater for those special customers, allowable types of payment terms must be defined and enforced (NET-30, COD, etc.). California sales tax in all its variations must also be contended with, along with the different categories of shipping orders (again, see Fig. 3.1).

We are also beginning to define attributes for our entities. From our interviewee we discover many details about how shipping orders are created and handled throughout the delivery process. Address information is dealt with quite differently for different subtypes of accounts. Salesmen, brokers, contact persons, tax eligibility of accounts, tax amount per order, freight charges, and much more is extracted. By examining existing column definitions and thoroughly inquiring with both our interviewees and workshop participants (some of whom are quite knowledgeable) on the meanings of those columns, we begin to form a picture of valid attributes. Of course, we're also able to eliminate some derived and obsolete columns, improving the quality of our evolving database specifications.

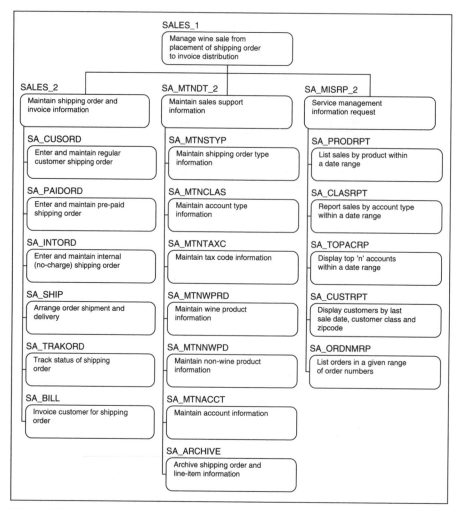

Figure 3.1 Analysis-Level Entity Relationship Diagram

Finally, by establishing these support or reference entities, we also identify future table mainte-nance functions. Our interviewee communicates details on the reports most commonly required by sales management. After this meeting we're able to return to CASE*Designer and CASE*Dictionary to fill out our function hierarchy and ERD as in Figures 3.2 and 3.1. Although we might find more functions on the first level of decomposition, in general we're beginning to look at breaking out the existing ones into more detail, and any further interviews will focus on accomplishing that. Figure 3.3 shows the *Function Definition Screen* where details such as "Frequency", "Response Needed", "Description", and "Notes" can be entered. (See Section 5.1 for more on "Response Needed".)

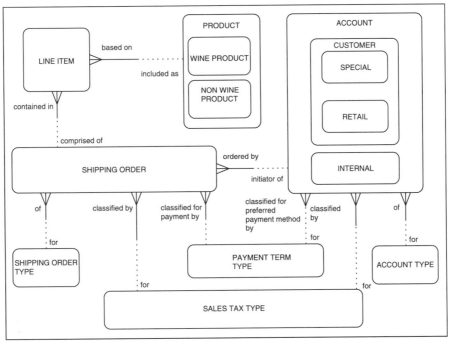

Figure 3.2 Analysis-level Function Hierarchy

Figure 3.3

Function Definition
Screen—Page 1

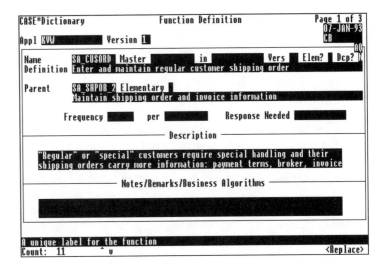

3.3 Reaching Elementary Functions and Avoiding Mechanisms

Successfully reaching (and not over-reaching) the elementary level of a function hierarchy requires practice. One useful way to do this is to determine how often a function generates useful data before it's completed. Thus, invoicing a customer is a good example of an elementary function because the invoice is the only piece of information generated by the process. But a function such as "Purchase Supplies" generates information at several points: first when a requisition is received, second when the item is ordered, then again when the item ordered is received, and finally if or when the received item is rejected and returned (see Appendix D). All these points represent decomposed elementary functions of "Purchase Supplies".

Another way to recognize needed decomposition is to look for substantial variations in types of information being collected under one function. In our analysis we find that "Enter and Maintain Shipping Order" needs to be split up into three elementary functions because KVW's different account subtypes require different processing. For example, we want to hold much more data about a "special" customer than about either a retail ("pre-paid") customer or an internal account. This means that the complexity of data-entry/maintenance forms and validation routines for these subtypes will vary widely.

Sometimes a function that has already been decomposed to an elementary level will be further broken up into smaller units that don't pass the criteria established above—that is, units that don't generate new information or are incomplete processes in themselves. This may be done to help document the steps involved in a complex elementary function. In doing so, however, it's useful to keep in mind how the *Default Application Designer* (DAD) selects functions to be defined as application modules. It creates a module definition for any function that is marked as elementary (see Fig. 3.3), so if we specify "Elem?" = "Y" for a function, the DAD ignores any further decomposition of it. Otherwise, by default it defines modules based on the lowest level (or "leaf") functions of a hierarchy.

Often, fragments of elementary functions will take the form of *mechanisms*, actions dependent on the technologies used. For example, it would be a mistake to decompose the function "Invoice customer for shipping order" into "Print Invoice" and "Mail invoice to customer". These are both mechanisms that describe *how* a function is performed, rather than *what* it is. In this case, if KVW had direct modem connections to all its customers, neither of these actions would be necessary in order to communicate an invoice to them.

In fact, mechanisms can appear at all levels of a function hierarchy, not just on an elementary level. For example, we could have incorrectly described "Maintain shipping order information" as "Maintain shipping order database in the computer". Some other examples of mechanisms are roles, job titles, organizations, equipment (in short, any names).

One major purpose for conducting our analysis as we do is to form models that will outlast the constantly changing methods of business operations. Mirroring only "what" a business does avoids focusing on those transient technologies and provides purer models that are conducive to examining all the options when planning IS changes or enhancements, whether they involve software, hardware, or manual systems. Such models also require less updating as circumstances change. During the design stage we take the "how" into consideration and automate our functions to the desired (and feasible) extent.

3.4   On Normalization

Up until now we've been pursuing a sort of quality assurance (QA) with regard to information processing (functions). Now we need to concern ourselves with QA on the data themselves. This is accomplished through the discipline of normalization. Much has been written on this subject, so we limit our discussion to a brief definition of the technique and the first three normal forms with examples.

Data normalization aims at eliminating redundancy of information in our database as well as ensuring that all required data are uniquely retrievable, that is, that we can always access every occurrence of the data we need as an individual row of a database table or as part of a row. A series of tests, each one more demanding than its predecessor, can be applied to determine the degree of normalization we've reached. In business information systems, data that have passed the "third normal form" test are generally considered to be adequately normalized. The three tests can be described as follows:

First Normal Form (1NF):

> Here we examine the attributes of our entities to ensure that each of them represents an "atomic value." This means that only one significant value of an attribute should be held in each occurrence of an entity. A typical example of failing to achieve the 1NF level is found in repeating groups, where an attribute recurs within one occurrence of an entity (such as attributes item1, item2, item3, etc.). This should be set up as an entity of its own (entity "Item"), establishing a "master/detail" relationship (one-to-many) with the entity from which it was removed.

Second Normal Form (2NF):

> Once we've resolved our data to a 1NF level, we can ask whether, as C.J. Date[1] puts it, "every nonkey attribute is fully dependent on the primary key." This applies to primary keys that are made up of several attributes, for example, a wine product that's uniquely identified by year, variety, and style (1986/Cabernet Sauvignon/Reserve). All attributes of this entity must depend on its complete key, otherwise they're entities themselves. Continuing our example, a description of the variety requires only part of the UID (variety) for its value. We would need to create an entity "Variety" with an identifier and description if our client wanted to keep track of that information.

---

[1]C.J.Date: *Database Systems,* Volume 1, Fourth Edition, Addison-Wesley, 1986

Third Normal Form (3NF):

> After our data have reached 2NF we need to ask whether our attributes are all intransitively dependent on the entity's unique identifier. An example of a transitive dependency would be the inclusion of the attribute "Customer Name" in the entity "Shipping Order". Although this attribute is dependent on the "Order Number" (Shipping Order's UID), that dependency is transitive, or indirect, occuring by way of the foreign key "Customer ID" and not intransitive, that is, solely in relationship to the unique identifier. In this case, "Customer Name" should belong only to the entity "Customer" before 3NF is achieved.

A skilled analyst will tend to achieve significant data normalization just through the process of building and refining ERDs. But each attribute and relationship still needs detailed examination in preparation for a high-quality database design.

3.5   More Details

As the next step in our workshop, one of the participants interviews the shipping manager. We want to verify that we have included all shipping-related entities and functions in our models. This conversation results in more additions to our ERD. We need to include "Warehouse" and "Warehouse Product" as entities (see Fig. 3.4). "Warehouse Product" functions as the intersection entity that resolves a many-to-many relationship between "Warehouse" and "Product" and contains inventory quantities by product and warehouse. This is our interface to the winery's inventory control system. We have decided not to include other shipping department duties (restocking warehouses and handling returned merchandise) in our project, both because they're less related to sales administration and because they won't be manageable within our time frame. However, in order to make the sample application work, we do need two more elementary functions to handle the maintenance of warehouse and warehouse product information. It's probably useful to emphasize again at this point how important this discipline of limiting a workshop's scope really is—it can make it or break it.

3.6   Refining Entities in CASE*Dictionary

Now we begin specifying volumes and synonyms and refining descriptions for our entities. We do this through CASE*Dictionary from the *Entity/Attribute Definition Screen* (see Figs. 3.5 and 3.6) under either the *Strategy Menu* or the *Analysis Data Requirements Menu*. Once we've entered entity details and initially defined their attributes, we use the *Attribute Definition Screen* to specify even more details regarding the attributes (see Fig. 3.7).

Figure 3.4
Entity Relationship
Diagram at the
End of Analysis

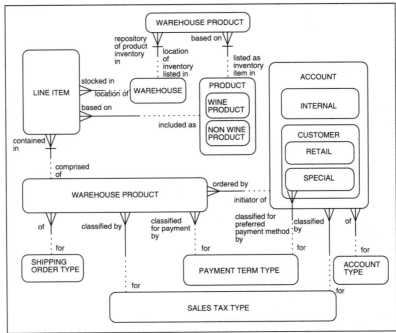

Because we have created our entities in CASE*Designer, the basic entity definitions are already in CASE*Dictionary. We can verify this by scrolling through the *Entity/Attribute Definition Screen.* CASE*Dictionary supplies a default "Short Name" and "Plural" of our entity name by truncating it for the first field and tagging an "S" onto it for the second. These may need to be modified. In a full-scale CASE project, the "Description" field would have been filled during strategy, but in our workshop all the following fields are still blank, awaiting our input.

Figure 3.5
Entity/Attribute
Definition Screen

```
CASE*Dictionary          Entity/Attribute Definition        Page 1 of 2
                                                            30-SEP-92
Appl KVW          Version 1  Owns Entity ? YES              CB
                                                               A0

    Name ACCOUNT                       Short Name ACCT      Type 1

  Plural ACCOUNTS                      Volumes -  Initial 780
                                                  Average
 Type of                                          Maximum
                                       Annual growth rate (%) 25

         ── Synonyms ──



         ── Description ──
  This provides default account information for a shipping order and
  serves as the super-type for customer and internal account informa-
  tion.


The name of an entity (a thing of significance)
Count:  1        v                                         <Replace>
```

Here we can also enter volumetric information to be used for sizing our database, including initial, average, and maximum values (number of occurences) for all our entities. Frequently, however, a maximum limit isn't appropriate (for example, with shipping orders or payment items). In these cases the annual growth rate percentage field can be used. For KVW, we often use 25% because this number was expressed during past interviews as a key performance indicator (KPI). On the other hand, an entity that defines a "type" for validation—such as "Shipping Order Type"—can actually be given a maximum volume since we know that there will always be a limited number of types. With all this information the database administrator (DBA) will later use the *Database Sizing Utility* to calculate the physical size of the database and its elements and choose an optimal way of implementing it.

Synonyms are optional but helpful for the clarification of industry terms that approximate one another (for example: "customer" and "client"). Only unique names for synonyms AND entities are allowed. If conflicts arise they point to areas where terms have been used ambiguously. The *System Glossary Report* can help clarify such areas by providing an overview of entities, synonyms, and their descriptions.

The contents of the "Description" block are our reasons for finding an entity important. The field's length is unlimited, so we can be as detailed as we want. No matter how complete and accurate our graphic models are, a few words of explanation about any crucial aspects of an entity, kept in an accessible repository, can prevent costly misunderstandings. Notes can be stored here on unresolved questions, allowing this field to become a kind of open forum on each entity's definition. This allows every team member to stay current with the project just by browsing in CASE*Dictionary.

3.7   Defining Attributes in CASE*Dictionary

On the second page of our *Entity/Attribute Definition Screen* (see Fig. 3.6) we begin entering the attributes we have arrived at for each entity. This page scrolls through all defined attributes of an entity, holding three basic attribute definitions at one time. We fill in the optionality, format, and length, flag our unique identifiers, and add notes for each attribute.

Figure 3.6
Entity/Attribute
Definition Screen—
Page 2

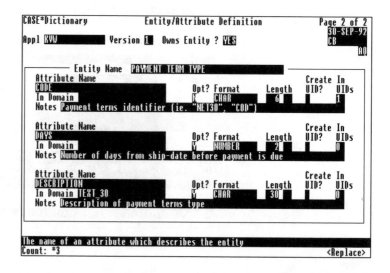

3.8   On Domains

The most efficient way to group attributes that have the same data definitions throughout an application is to use domains. These can be defined on the spot (*Entity/Attribute Definition Screen* or *Attribute Definition Screen*) by entering a domain name for an attribute. They can also be created directly in the *Domain Definition Screen*, which is accessible through the *Strategy Menu* or the *Analysis Data Requirements Menu*. A third way is to define them on a column level during the design stage through the *Table* or the *Column Definition Screen*.

Once a domain is created, just entering the domain name in the appropriate screen field will automatically bring up the format or datatype and the length associated with it. It is also possible to define a default value and/or a set of valid values for each domain on the *Domain Definition Screen* (however, "Null/Value" and "Derivation" are not currently in use). Later, during the build stage, you can move a domain's set of valid values into the CASE*Dictionary table CG_REF_CODES by running the utility *Update Reference Code Tables*. From there your application can access it, and CASE*Generator for SQL*Forms/ SQL*Menu will enforce validation while automatically creating a List-of-Values pop-up window for all columns in that domain. If your valid set of values changes, you'll need to run this utility again to update CG_REF_CODES, but it isn't necessary to generate your application again. (A sigh of relief is often heard at this point.)

If an attribute participates in a domain, then the *Default Database Design Utility* will forward the related information to a column created from it. Domains do more than reduce the work of entering details. Any time you decide to change some part of a domain's definition, that change will be reflected in all attributes or columns of that type after the utilities *Update Attributes in a Domain* or *Update Columns in a Domain* are run. If you want to standardize data definitions across your application, this is the way to go.

After using the *Entity/Attribute Definition Screen* initially to set up attribute definitions throughout our application, we begin to work more from the *Attribute Definition Screen* (see Fig. 3.7). This is a two-page form where all the details we have already defined are displayed, along with fields for many others that can now be entered. These include usage percentage, security parameters, default and high values, validation rules, and an unlimited description block. By the end of the analysis stage we need to have as many of these details in place as possible in order to provide a solid foundation for our database and application designs.

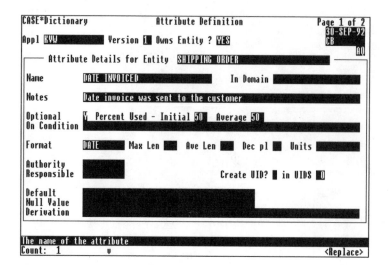

Figure 3.7
Attribute Definition
Screen—Page 1

3.9   Unique Identifiers

Each occurrence of an entity requires one unique identifier (UID). Once we've settled on our entity and attribute definitions, we can enter "Y" in the field "Create UID?" on the *Entity/Attribute Definition Screen* or the *Attribute Definition Screen*. This is a shortcut to populate the *Unique Identifier Screen* (see Fig. 3.8) where, of course, we can define and modify UIDs directly.

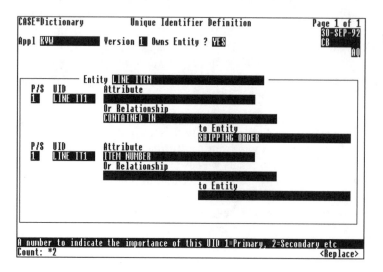

Figure 3.8
Unique Identifier Screen

A unique identifier can be built out of one or more attributes and/or one or more relationships. To define an attribute or a relationship as part of a UID, we can pick up the appropriate name from a List of Values. ORACLE can enforce uniqueness for up to sixteen elements. CASE*Dictionary supplies a default name for each UID.

Sometimes we find several "candidate keys" that could be used to identify an occurence of an entity uniquely. We keep track of them using a number in the "P/S" field to indicate their relative importance.

3.10   Business Units

Since organizations are often divided into groups or departments, or by physical location, CASE*Dictionary provides a means of defining such units (as we did during the strategy stage: see the end of Section 2.12). In our case, we define only one business unit, SALES, and associate it with all our elementary functions except "Maintain tax code information" and "Maintain wine product information" (see Fig. 3.9). Both these functions and their associated data actually belong to other groups in KVW, the tax code maintenance to accounting, and the wine product maintenance to production and inventory. We needed to create them during the workshop to validate the data-entry of shipping orders.

Figure 3.9
Business Unit Definition
Screen—Page 2

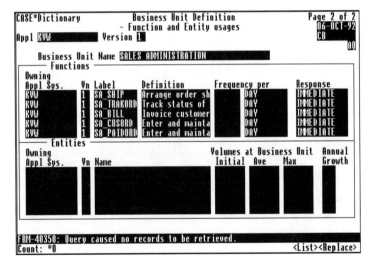

Later, when using the *Default Menu Design Utility*, the connection between business units and elementary functions will provide input for a first cut of our menu definitions.

3.11   Using Dataflow Diagrams

Our client specifically requested that we include Dataflow Diagrams (DFD) in this study, though we have successfully conducted similar workshops without using them. CASE*Designer provides a Dataflow Diagrammer within its GUI environment that works in a way similar to the Entity Diagrammer. With this technique it is possible to model the movement of data (dataflow) between functions (or processes) and the input and output of the system being analyzed (external entity). We also model the dataflow between functions and a "datastore," that is, a repository where the dataflow comes to rest. However, a flow between an external entity and a datastore is "illegal" since it would mean that the entity had direct access to internal data. DFDs show neither the processing within a function nor *when* that processing is executed, but do require that all the incoming data be used to produce the outgoing dataflow.

Since a DFD that included all levels of detail would be unreadable, we begin by building a high-level model that shows our system as one function with its input and output. Such a "context diagram" (see Fig. 3.10) can be very helpful during the process of establishing a CASE project's scope and visualizing interfaces to the outside world (for example, other information systems, the IRS, the bank, other companies, people). This perspective is not available from other CASE tools.

Achieving a context diagram with the Dataflow Diagrammer is a bit challenging, however. To create a diagram with dataflows as they're indicated in Figure 3.10, it's necessary first to define a "dummy" root function, open the diagram at that level, copy SALES_1 into it, draw dataflows between SALES_1 and the other functions and the external entity, and finally select SALES_1 and re-open the diagram "down." This is rather cumbersome, but we understand the problem is being addressed.

A context DFD is a typical usage at the strategy level, but during analysis the Dataflow Diagrammer offers another valuable service. By using it to model dataflows to and from elementary functions, we can readily observe which of those functions either receives no data or sends none to other functions, datastores, or external entities. Finding such a function usually doesn't mean it's redundant, but simply that we've failed to understand its use. A similar quality check can be performed for each datastore: is there at least one incoming dataflow to create its content and one outgoing flow which uses the stored data? Another point to check is whether an elementary function has many incoming and outgoing dataflows. Could they be merged—or is the function we're looking at not really elementary? In the Dataflow Diagrammer, a DFD can be created for any level of a function hierarchy, but only for that level (see Fig. 3.11). At this stage we can also check "level balancing"—whether a lower level decomposition has lost any dataflows from a higher level.

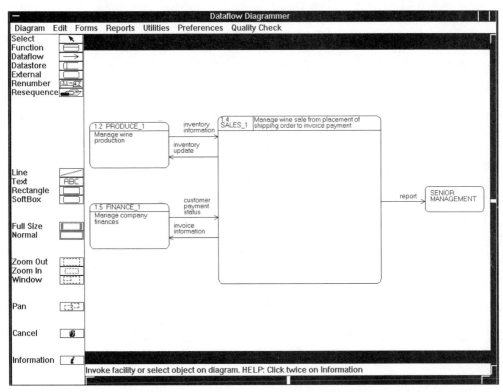

Figure 3.10 Context Diagram

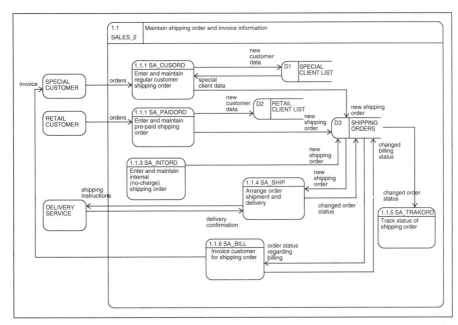

Figure 3.11 SALES Dataflow Diagram

When drawing DFDs it is possible to copy in business functions, and we might also want to try copying entities. But the entities of an ERD and those of a DFD are two different things. The first one, called an *internal entity*, represents the data we need to keep track of; while the second *external entity* is a terminator for a dataflow. This means that the only entities we can copy into a DFD are those external entities we have already created somewhere else in the Dataflow Diagrammer. Unfortunately, all entities are accessed via the same CASE*Dictionary synonym, so their names have to be unique and they all show up when, for example, the *Entity/Attribute Definition Screen* is queried or when the Matrix Diagrammer (see Fig. 3.12) is used for cross-checking. In our example, 'Special Customer' and 'Retail Customer' are external entities, while the account subtypes "Special" and "Retail" are internal ones. Logically, these two quite distinct concepts should be referenced in separate tables. We hope that this design flaw will be corrected in the next version of CASE*Dictionary.

3.12 Cross-checking with the Matrix Diagrammer

The Matrix Diagrammer is our primary cross-checking tool. We can relate many different elements to one another: business objectives, key performance indicators, entities, functions, business units, tables, and modules, to name just a few. It also works with elements defined under "User Extensibility" in CASE*Dictionary (see Appendix A). Here are some examples of applying the Matrix Diagrammer:

- Sorting entities by volume and functions by frequency to show which ones are the most critical in an application,

- Using entity/business unit and function/business unit diagrams as a basis for decisions about distributed databases and distributed processing,

- Using the relationships between tables and modules to get impact analysis information, and

- Using the Function/Entity and Function/Attribute Matrices to provide completeness and consistency checks on whether each entity and attribute can pass through a complete life cycle of being created, used, and archived or deleted.

This last point is the one we concentrate on during our workshop. We begin by running the *Generate Candidate Function/Entity Matrix Utility* from the *Analysis Utilities Menu* in CASE*Dictionary. This utility matches words in functions, entities, and their synonyms via SQL*TextRetrieval and creates default "Other" usages in the intersections between them.

To set up the diagram we click on "Open" in the "Diagram" pull-down menu. Using a series of pop-up windows we select "Entity" for the column side of the matrix and "Business Function" for the row side. Now the Matrix Diagrammer creates our default matrix with part of the "Comment" field in the intersection. Once it is displayed, we use the "Preferences" pull-down menu to resize the column and row descriptions so that they're legible. Then we delete intersections to everything but the elementary functions by clicking on the appropriate intersections and choosing the "Delete" option from the "Edit" pull-down menu.

Next comes a rather cumbersome part of our task: that of calling up the properties we want displayed in each matrix intersection. We first select "Intersection" from the "Properties to be displayed" option under "Preferences" and choose, say, "Create" from the pop-up list. This means we want to see whether each entity provides at least one way for its occurences to be created (or, as we might say in the design stage, we are "having rows inserted into the database"). No changes will be displayed until we re-open the diagram. Usually at this point we would also want to display other properties of an intersection. To do this, we select "Properties to be appended" (*not* "displayed") and go through the same procedure for the properties "retrieve", "update", and "delete" (altogether forming the acronym CRUD). "Archive" and "Other" are also available. This requires a lot of clicking, but when the properties needed have been appended, we can re-open the diagram to get our desired image. An optional "iconic" display mode is also available (see Fig. 3.12), which requires much less effort to produce but also supplies less information.

In the case of the "elementary functions to entities" diagram, the labors we've endured are worth the pain because we now have an overview of our CRUD relationships that we can efficiently check and correct (see Fig. 3.13). Deciding on the types of data usages required by a function for each entity is a painstaking job and should be done with care, though corrections can be made during the module design stage. One point worth mentioning here regards the handling of super/subtype entity structures: define CRUD usages only for the lowest level of subtypes. For example, in Figure 3.13, usages are entered only for SPECIAL, RETAIL, and INTERNAL in our ACCOUNT entity structure, while ACCOUNT and CUSTOMER are left blank. This is because sub-types inherit all attributes of their super-types.

All changes we make to our matrix diagram are directly updated in CASE*Dictionary. To accomplish this we need to double-click on an intersection and enter its new function/entity usage into a pop-up window. No typing directly into the intersection is allowed. Of course, we don't close a diagram without some consideration: we have to go through the whole procedure of displaying properties every time we open one.

Alternatively, we could validate and refine entities used by each elementary function on page 2 of the *Function Definition Screen* in CASE*Dictionary (see Fig. 3.14). Once we've completed our checks on the proper function/entity usage we proceed by running the *Create Function/Attribute Matrix Utility* from the *Analysis Utilities Menu*. This utility forwards the entity usage to the attributes. We could refine these display, insert, retrieve, update, and nullify usages either in the Matrix Diagrammer or again on page two of the *Function Definition Screen* (see Fig. 3.14). It may be useful to emphasize here that both CASE*Dictionary and CASE*Designer access the same information, so that changes made in one tool are reflected in the other.

In our workshop, however, we've postponed any decisions on how attributes are used by each elementary function until the design stage. Then the module design is closely followed by implementation and, through reiterating the cycle of design, generate, and test, we'll develop our application. This approach is useful in a workshop because we want to explore the possibilities of the CASE generators.

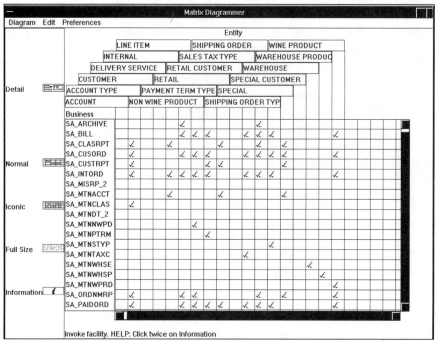

Figure 3.12 Iconic Matrix Diagram

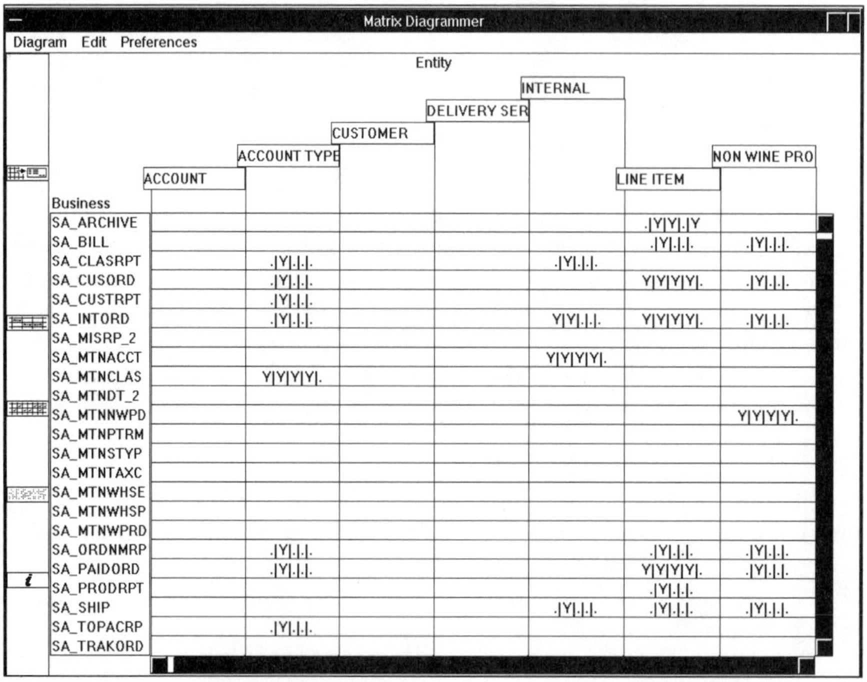

Figure 3.13 Function/Entity Matrix

Figure 3.14

Function Definition
Screen—Page 2

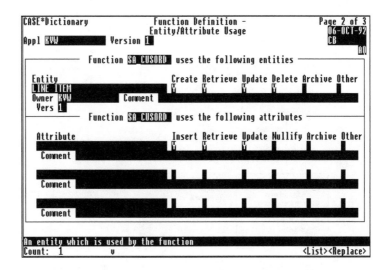

On page one of the *Function Definition Screen* (see Fig. 3.3) there is one field we need to consider carefully right now. This is the "Response Needed" parameter with two allowable values: IMMEDIATE and OVERNIGHT. Depending on the CRUD usages we've established, the *Default Application Designer* (DAD) will later use our entry here to define types of modules to be based on our elementary functions. For more information on how these factors affect DAD, see Section 5.1, "Creating Module Definitions."

All the detailed work of our analysis will be carried forward into and through the following development stages and will help form the basis on which we generate forms, reports, and menus. A sketch that we've developed for our workshops provides a rough overview of this (see Fig. 3.15). During Strategy and Analysis, elements and their properties (for example, entities, elementary functions, and business units) have been defined and their associations to one another have been recorded through the Matrix Diagrammer and the *Business Unit Definition Screen* (page 2). During Design we'll run the *Default Database, Module*, and *Menu Design* utilities to create Data and Module definitions in the CASE*Dictionary. During the implementation these are used by the generators to create our relational database and all the on-line forms, menus, and reports which our final application comprises.

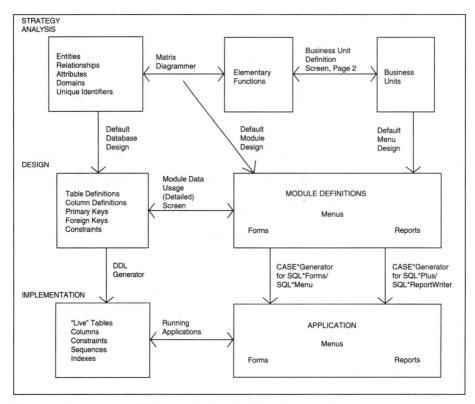

Figure 3.15 Overview of Elements during the Development Process

3.13   Reports during Strategy and Analysis

One of the strengths of Oracle's CASE tools lies in their extensive reporting capabilities. This is particularly important when using a method where so much depends on iterative feedback and synthesized information. Documents to which we can repeatedly refer and that can be continuously updated and corrected provide an effective basis for communicating with users, for example, through the reports *System Glossary, Entities and their Attributes,* and *Attributes in a Domain.* Some reports such as *Function Hierarchy* or *Entity Relationship Diagram Details* are simply reformulations of our models in a more textual (and sometimes a more detailed) form. In this sense, printed diagrams and reports are of a piece, complementing one another, each contributing to our understanding of the whole. Another use of reports is for quality assurance and cross-checking: *Entities with no Attributes, . . . no Relationships,* or *. . . no Unique Identifier* will require some attention. This group is easily accessible under the *Strategy & Analysis Quality Checks Menu* (see Fig. 3.16).

Figure 3.16
Strategy & Analysis
Quality Checks Menu

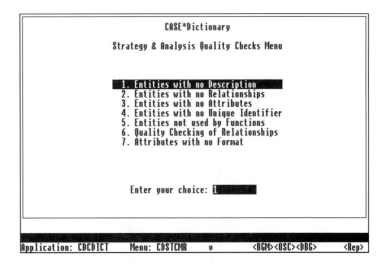

CASE*Dictionary provides over 100 pre-defined reports, but it also supports the creation of customized reports. This can be done by establishing a "User Defined Reporter" (see Section 2.11, "Access to CASE"). Knowing the password of this userid allows access to CASE views that are described in the CASE*Dictionary Reference Guide.

3.14   On Feedback Sessions

Feedback sessions are intrinsic to the reiterated interviewing process, and even in our time-starved workshop we've been regularly returning to users at all levels for feedback on our models. We've communicated our findings back to them, using subset ERDs, function hierarchies, and DFDs as well as printed reports when appropriate. Models of data and functions specifically known to interviewees are easier for them to understand than our "standard" models, designed to reflect functional areas or business units. Additionally, such subset models can enrich the analytical process by revealing unexpected perspectives.

The interviewing skills we employed to extract this information in the first place must be even more rigorously applied in feedback sessions. The first time around we were primarily trying to listen and ask the right questions, but in a feedback session we're returning to the user with our well-organized models. And because they're in print, we'll all be tempted to accept these authoritative-looking documents at face value. We need to remember that these diagrams are communication tools and make sure we've taken nothing for granted (especially if the analyst already has experience in the business area being discussed). For example, we need to read out each relationship in our ERDs, emphasizing "*must* be" or "one-and-only-one"—always, etc.

In a large-scale CASE study, the end of each stage is marked by a "checkpoint" or "land-mark" session. These are prepared for by checking the completeness and consistency of models and carefully planning the event. Here are some points to remember:

- Invite the attendees well ahead of time.

- Prepare the room, equipment, refreshments, and your materials and hand-outs.

- Practice your presentation.

- Try to avoid interruptions.

- Manage time well:

    –schedule highlights to sustain attention, and

    –dynamically reschedule if necessary.

- Ensure that everyone can follow the modeling techniques being used.

- Make sure that someone is taking detailed notes.

There are two different kinds of checkpoint sessions. In the first one, you meet with your user expert team—those people you've been interviewing on a more detailed-analysis level. Together with them you take a final shot at refining your business models before taking them to senior management. The intention is not only to improve them, but also to raise everyone's understanding of the business as a whole. An added benefit of this event is that it further reinforces the tendency of these users to take ownership of the study and its resulting applications. Of course, you'll also need to reach a final agreement on the accuracy and completeness of the models and, as with all feedback sessions, any errors found in analysis at this point will require that those models be consolidated, and that agreed changes be sent out after the meeting.

Once you've validated your models and finished all the other tasks associated with this stage (see the Analysis section of the Introduction), the second type of session is arranged: a presentation to senior management. In this one- or two-hour meeting you first ensure that you've understood the primary objectives of the company by describing where the business is, where its decision makers want it to go, and how they intend to get it there. Again, business goals, critical success factors, and key performance indicators are often the appropriate terms with which to address senior management. You'll also present your final high-level models, an implementation plan and, possibly, alternative plans, each with a cost/benefit summary. Your objective at this stage is to obtain a commitment from management to the project's continuation.

As implied above, we are not required, nor do we have time for, events on this scale during our project. Here we are accountable for something else: a functioning application at the workshop's end.

4

Data Design and Implementation

The primary deliverables of an analysis stage are detailed IS specifications for the functional area being studied, that is, "what" its information needs are. During the design stage, powerful utilities help us transform these requirements into detailed definitions for implementation: "how" the information needs are to be met. In a workshop setting, we design and create our database before beginning with application modules.

4.1   Preparing for the Design of a Relational Database

We are now into the sixth day of our workshop and are ready to apply our analysis specifications to designing our database. Our goal is to optimize system performance based on our understanding of how the data are to be used. CASE*Method supports the simultaneous design of data and processes (modules), but our workshop experience suggests a slightly different approach. We've found that software engineers often prefer to design and implement the database first, especially when this corresponds with their accustomed development sequence. Then, in a separate step, we carry out the iterative process of designing modules with our table definitions.

Taking those "ideal" database specifications from our analysis-level models, we begin by brainstorming together with our team members on how to implement those models for high performance and efficient use. If we carry out this task properly, we get the additional benefit of re-verifying our models for completeness. Under the pressure of a workshop timetable, some details may have slipped by. Now, with closer scrutiny, they can be included.

We first decide how we want to implement our entities as database tables. To aid our thinking on this topic, we examine our current ERD (see Fig. 3.4) where we see two super/subtype entity combinations. Our own general premise is that, if there's no significant reason not to (such as a distributed database), it's best to implement a super/subtype entity as one table for reasons of performance and simplicity. However, each instance should be carefully analyzed before this determination is made. Some factors to consider are:

- **Unique identifiers**: Are they defined on the level of the super- or subtypes?

- **Relationships**: Are there many common relationships?

- **Attributes**: How are they distributed between super- and subtypes? Are there mandatory attributes for subtypes?

- **Validation**: Do super- and subtypes require similar validation?

- **Usage**: Are super- and subtypes retrieved and/or manipulated together?

- **Size**: Are there constraints due to the sizes of tables and their storage media?

We begin with the "Account" entity, concentrating on the actual differences between the subtypes "Customer", divided into "Special" and "Retail", and "Internal" (see Section 3.1 for details). Additionally, our sponsoring user has asked us to use a six-character short name called "Customer ID" as the UID for all accounts, but we observe that this reflects "flat-file" implementation with its limited querying capability. In fact, it now seems that retail customers shouldn't be given such a sort-and-search mechanism and that it's only useful for special customers and internal accounts (i.e., with twenty "Smith"s on the retail list, descriptive short names will soon be used up, so a query on "Smith" bringing a subset of rows is more suitable).

As a result of this examination, we decide that "Accounts" should have a numeric UID and that the subtypes "Special" and "Internal" should have unique short names (six characters) for compatibility with the existing system and for controlled report sorting of customers with company names (e.g., "The Best in the West Restaurant" becomes "BESTWE"). We also realize that the differences in required data among the subtypes were emphasized during analysis by users who lacked experience with relational databases and assumed that address and invoicing columns containing null values would take a large amount of disk space. However, the ORACLE RDBMS stores only actual data (plus some overhead). It now seems clear that we can implement "Accounts" as one table.

Our other super/subtype structure is "Product", which we've divided into "Wine" and "Non Wine" (see Fig. 3.4). As we look more closely at these entities we notice a set of facts quite different from the ones we've just confronted with "Accounts". For one thing, the products have only one attribute, "description", in common, but each subtype has several attributes of its own. It also appears that "Wine" really belongs to the production and inventory department and contains product-related data that are relevant to sales and shipping. In fact, sales only has "read" privileges on the product ID (the UID) but can update the description and price categories for each product. "Non Wine", on the other hand, is of virtually no interest to production or inventory and represents a limited assortment of items occasionally sold to customers, such as corkscrews and gift-wrapping services. The inventory department currently doesn't even track nonwine stock, which is kept in one storage room adjoining the sales offices.

So our database implementation based on the "Product" structure will be very different from what we decided to do with "Account". Of course, our ERD doesn't include the new information, so we remodel this subset of our project as seen in Figure 4.1 and Appendix D. Clearly, we need to create two separate entities and two tables, NON_WINE_PRODUCTS and WINE_PRODUCTS, primarily for reasons of ownership.

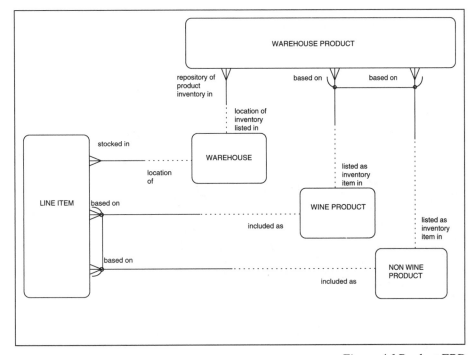

Figure 4.1 Product ERD

4.2   On Denormalizing

Designing a database for high performance raises the question of denormalizing. A trade-off decision has to be made between faster access and duplicated data that multiply storage requirements and data integrity rules. To *denormalize* simply means to reverse the process of normalizing data. For example, we might duplicate a column into a second table if it's so often required there that accessing it through a foreign key significantly degrades performance. Factors such as number of tables in a join operation, number of rows in a table, and frequency of use and of repeated calculations influence performance and need to be considered in our decision. In our project, we store the derived line-item price for order items since this price doesn't change once an order is entered. The need to support different business locations can also justify denormalizing, for example, where an entire duplicate table is needed at a remote location to reduce long-distance IOs. Again, by denormalizing we lose some of the benefits of centrally stored relational data and introduce more complex updating logic, so it's a step that should be carefully measured.

4.3   Creating Table and Tablespace Definitions

Now that we've decided on how to map entities to tables, we use CASE*Dictionary to begin creating those table definitions. From the *Data Design Utilities Menu* under the *Design Menu* we select the *Fastpath Table Mapping Screen* (see Fig. 4.2). Here we only need to press COMMIT after moving the cursor to each entity that should become a table. We need to be sure not to COMMIT on the indented subtypes of "Special", "Internal", and "Retail", since they will all be part of the ACCOUNTS table. We also have to watch out for external entities defined for our context DFD. Unfortunately, though they have nothing to do with tables, they are still on our entity list.

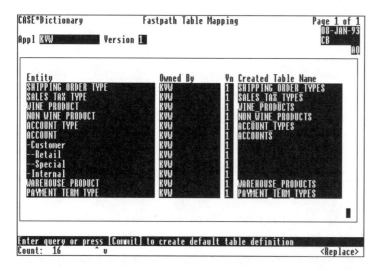

Figure 4.2

Fastpath Table
Mapping Screen

Our next decision is whether to create a special tablespace for our tables. If none is defined, either the default "SYSTEM" tablespace or the default tablespace assigned to the user will be utilized. The DBA in our group has become very interested in creating a special tablespace because all objects belonging to our application will be stored there, providing benefits for backup and recovery. So we decide to create a tablespace called "KVWTABS". To do this, we select the *Tablespace Definition Screen* from the *DBA Options Menu*. There we define our tablespace as seen in Figure 4.3. Note that under "Datafile Specification" we've defined a name "c:\oracle6\dbs\kvwtabs.ora" and given it five megabytes of disk space, which is an estimate based on our client's current database size. This entry is a shortcut that forwards our physical file definition to the *File Definition Screen*.

Figure 4.3
Tablespace Definition
Screen

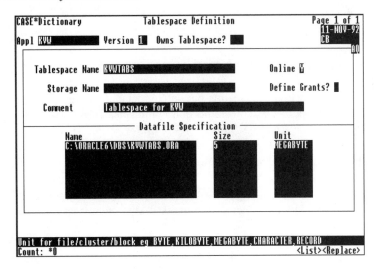

Now we can proceed to the *Table Definition Screen* under the *Database Design Menu* (see Fig. 4.4). Because we used the *Fastpath Table Mapping Screen* to map entities to tables, we have a first cut of our table definitions available by general query.

Figure 4.4
Table Definition Screen

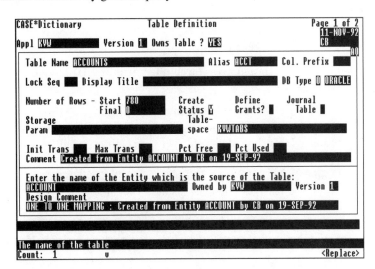

Before continuing on to create a default database design, we alter one field in every record that scrolls on this screen: "Col. Prefix" (column prefix). In all cases where the client's naming conventions don't require it, we recommend deleting the data in this field because they are used as prefixes for all column names, which generally seems redundant (unless ORACLE-reserved words have been used as attribute names). On the other hand, if the client wants to use the prefix, this is the right time to verify that the system has selected a suitable one from the table name. In cases where table names are identical for the first four characters (i.e., WAREHOUSES and WAREHOUSE_PRODUCTS), the system doesn't create a prefix, thus avoiding duplication. If desired, the "Display Title" to be viewed as a block heading on screens and a group heading on reports can also be added now. In our case, we want to enter "KVWTABS" as the "Tablespace". We can successfully do this only because we have already defined it in the *Tablespace Definition Screen* (see above).

4.4 Default Database Design

We are ready to begin creating our default database design, which means defining columns and keys and, optionally, constraints and comments. To do this we choose the *Default Database Design* option from the *Data Design Utilities Menu*. This is a batch process that runs from a command line and first offers us the options "V"alidate, "I"nsert, and "R"eplace. We always start by validating, which doesn't insert any definitions into the CASE tables but produces a screen report and/or print-out of those definitions. When asked to select tables for the design, we enter "%" for all of them. We want to study this report to see what kinds of warnings or errors the utility has diagnosed from our design. Some messages we encounter are:

> **Precision not defined hence default used**—usually for integers, such as sequence numbers. "Precision," or decimal places, which are mandatory for NUMBER datatypes, have been defined as the default: zeroes (0).

> **No attributes found for this entity**—this generally means either that the entity is actually an attribute of another entity or simply that we forgot to define attributes during analysis.

> **Relationship from sub-type—foreign key will be NULL**—this occurs with optional foreign key relationships.

> **Relationship in arc—foreign key will be NULL**—basically the same situation as the last one.

> **No intersection tables found**—this means we've successfully resolved all many-to-many relationships in our model; otherwise, if the utility (looking at all tables) finds a many-to-many relationship between entities, it will create a default intersection table.

The *Default Database Design Utility* turns attributes into columns, unique identifiers into primary keys, and resolves relationships into foreign key columns. When we look at an ERD, we can picture that a table based on an entity at the "Many" end of a one-to-many relationship will be supplied with a column for storing the foreign key (the primary key of a related table). In a 1:1 relationship it (theoretically) doesn't matter which entity holds the foreign key, since it is a

completely symmetrical relationship. As mentioned above, an "M:M" (many-to-many) relationship can be resolved into an intersection table. So here we see why CASE*Method requests
that foreign keys not be included as attributes—they would be duplicated and we would have
to take care of referential integrity.

Sometimes the *Default Database Design Utility* cannot resolve a relationship because it hasn't
found a table definition from which to take the primary key (it is currently not smart enough to
look ahead at the list of tables still to be worked with). Instead, it creates a column definition
called [table-name]_!MANUAL to accommodate the foreign key. Seeing "!MANUAL" on the
report is a red flag indicating that this definition needs to be resolved. This is reinforced by the
fact that the "!" cannot be used in ORACLE object names.

The warnings and errors we get on our report provide a good opportunity to put our team to
work checking them out and resolving them. When we have satisfactorily validated the design
we can run the utility using the "I"nsert option, which loads the column definitions into
CASE*Dictionary. Later, if we want to add new column definitions or change existing ones,
we'll use the "R"eplace option. Its name is a bit misleading because it doesn't actually delete
existing definitions, but instead allows their length, optionality, and datatype to be altered. If
we want to change a column name, for example, we first have to delete the old record manually. Then we can re-run this utility for a particular table or enter the new column definitions
manually (which might be faster for small changes).

4.5   Creating Sequence Definitions

We are almost ready to take on the task of defining columns in detail, but before we do it's
necessary to define *sequences*. These are database objects used to generate and increment numbers automatically, generally used for primary key values. We define sequences for three tables
in our workshop: ACCOUNTS, SHIPPING_ORDERS, and WAREHOUSES. From the
Database Design Menu we can select the *Sequence Definition Screen* to define our sequences.
As Figure 4.5 indicates, this is a fairly straightforward job. There are, however, a couple of
decisions we have to make here. The field "Order?" with a value "Y"es specifies that the
sequence numbers should be generated in the order in which users request them. The default is
"N"o, which means the order is arbitrary.

Then we need to think about "*caching*." If the default of "20" is accepted for this field, twenty
sequence numbers will be stored in memory, considerably improving performance in an active
multi-user environment. The risk is that of losing those numbers in a system crash (or even in
an orderly shutdown if they're in memory at the time) and creating a "hole" in our record
sequence that could violate auditing constraints. Although our application is designed to function in a multi-user setting, performance considerations do not outweigh this risk, and we
choose not to cache multiple numbers.

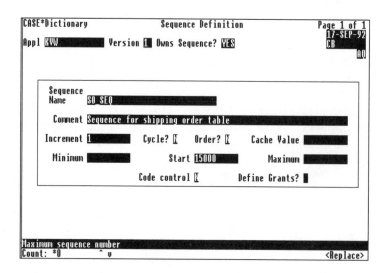

Figure 4.5
Sequence Definition
Screen

Generally, the "Code control" field at the bottom of this screen should contain the value "N". If "Y" is entered, no automatic sequence will be created for this definition. Instead, the "Code Control Sequence Definitions" block on the *CASE*Generator for Reference Tables Screen* will be flagged to create a special table for sequencing. This system can guarantee no holes in the sequence, but does present other potential problems (see Section 4.13 below for details).

4.6   A Detailed Look at Column Definitions

Turning back to the *Table Definition Screen*, we proceed to page 2 (see Fig. 4.7) where our newly created column definitions await us. They were derived from attributes when the *Default Database Design Utility* was run. We use our detailed data analysis to tailor this default design into one more closely fitted to user requirements. We could also work with these definitions from the *Column Definition Screen* (see Fig. 4.6) under the *Table Columns and Keys Menu*.

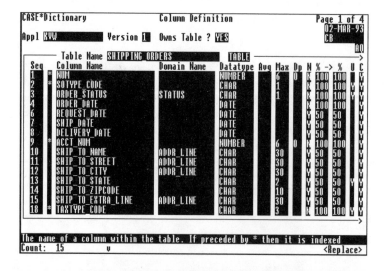

Figure 4.6
Column Definition
Screen—Page 1

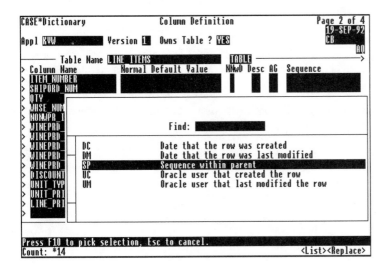

Figure 4.7
Column Definition
Screen—Page 2

The task of carefully examining and entering four pages of column definitions for each table might appear somewhat formidable at first. An inexperienced user would do well to start with the less complex tables. These can be quickly located on the current ERD where the simpler, low-volume entities are usually found at the bottom or to the right of the model (that is, if it was designed according to the "crows fly south and east" principle, explained in Section 2.14). We find it efficient first to refine column definitions of one or two tables together with the whole team for training. Then we break up the work among several members, where possible assigning our designers to data definitions they'd use or be responsible for on the job.

Oracle provides detailed explanations of most definition components in their *CASE*Dictionary Reference Guide*, so another tutorial isn't required at this point, but here are some tips about the process. Remember that whatever is defined on pages one and two of the *Column Definition Screen* is used directly by the CASE generators and cannot be overridden elsewhere, so be sure you've got it right here.

PAGE ONE

Datatype—the field with this name on page one is related to the storage of data while the one on page three is for display.

Uppercase—refers to the form of storage and default display, so think carefully about this. For example, sometimes it's better to store a description in uppercase to ensure uniformity of data entry and ease of retrieval, whereas in a "comments" field a free-text format is usually more suitable.

PAGE TWO

Normal Default Value—a common use for this is to insert, for example, the current date into an "order date" column when a new row is being created. To do this, enter SYSDATE or $$DATE$$ here.

Descriptor—this column helps identify a row in a table. The CASE generators uses this information in two ways to define implicitly:

1) links to look-up fields (see Section 5.5 and Fig. 5.13). Name and description fields are often defined as descriptors to be displayed on a list of values along with the primary key.

2) "copy context" fields (for an example, see Section 5.7, and Figs. 5.22 and 5.23).

AG—automatically generated values. We use "SP" (Sequence within Parent) for our line-item number, which, together with the shipping-order number, forms the unique identifier for the LINE_ITEMS table (see Fig. 4.7).

Sequence—only sequence names that have already been defined in the *Sequence Definition Screen* are allowed here.

PAGE THREE

Length—the display length of a field should be large enough for a format mask. When a NUMBER field is being formatted, the length might need to be increased by two (for +/- sign and decimal place) while RMONEY fields require one extra byte (see Section 5.3).

Format Mask—useful for formatting numbers, especially money fields, but we suggest not using it to define formats for your date columns. Since these are usually uniform throughout an application, it makes more sense to define a format as your "user preference" using the Default Date Display Format (DFTDTE) in CASE*Generator for SQL*Forms (see Section 5.7).

PAGE FOUR

Normal Prompt

1) As they're created by the *Default Database Design Utility*, they're not always suitable for form and report prompts, so check and refine them all.

2) Don't add a colon (:) or greater-than sign (>) here for screen prompts. If one of these is to be a standard convention, define it as a user preference in CASE generators.

3) Make sure that no prompts are left blank so that a field can always be identified when it appears on a form or report by accident.

Hint—these are carried forward from attribute descriptions, so verify that they're still appropriate. They will be forwarded again by the CASE*Generator for SQL*Forms to be used as hint text on form message lines.

4.7   Column Validation and Derivation

From the Column Definition screen we can jump directly to the *Column Validation and Derivation Screen* by using a *hot key*.

On Hot Keys

The hot keys (usually [Block Menu]) are defined on some CASE*Dictionary screens to allow direct access to a related screen without going through the menus. A list of hot key connections follows:

FROM SCREEN	TO SCREEN
Table Definition	Table Key Constraints Definition
Column Definition	Column Validation and Derivation
Module Definition	Module Network
CASE Generator	Module Data Usage (detailed)
Module Data Usage	Module Data Usage (detailed)
Module Planning	Module Network
Candidate Module Specification Acceptance	Module Definition

Pressing [Exit] returns the previous screen.

We want to use the *Column Validation and Derivation Screen* to establish valid values for all columns that require them, either as a list of values or as a range. Figure 4.8 shows an example of the kind of entry we perform on several columns in our database. Here, allowed values for the column ORDER_STATUS in the SHIPPING_ORDERS table are defined. This data is added to CASE*Dictionary reference tables to be used by CASE generators. If we were establishing a range of values, we'd use the "Value" field to enter the low value, then "High Value" as indicated. If allowed values have been entered either at the attribute or domain level, they won't be visible on this screen. We could run the reports *Domain Definition* (CDDOMDEF.LIS) and *Attribute Definition* (CDATTDEF.LIS) to make sure that we don't duplicate our work. However, any values or ranges defined here will override all previously defined values.

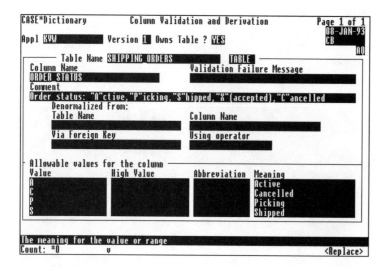

Figure 4.8
Column Validation and
Derivation Screen

If we'd defined any columns as result of denormalization in our workshop, this would be the screen to use for entering their source: table, column name, and foreign key (see Section 4.2, On Denormalizing). This information is essential for documentation.

We now begin defining expressions for the derivation of columns. To do this, we position the cursor on any field within the first block and press [Edit Text] which displays a pop-up window (see Fig. 4.9) with the default "Text Type" of "Derivation Expression". We could select any of several other text types here by pressing the [List of Values] key, but we'll start with the default, using the example below: the LINE_PRICE column in the table LINE_ITEMS. This column is derived from a formula using several other columns in the same table, so our derivation expression is constructed as a DECODE expression, specifying two similar formulae depending on the value of UNIT_TYPE (one for "B"ottle, the other for the rest).

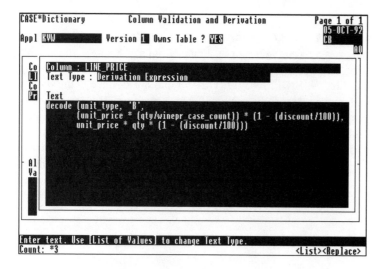

Figure 4.9
Derivation Expression
for a Column

4.8   On Edit Text

The list of values for Edit Text offers:

Description—specifies the purpose of an object such as a column, key, table, or module.

Notes—used for change history and other development remarks.

Derivation Expression—an SQL expression (see example above) that defines how the column has derived its value. Since the field into which the expression is entered has a free format, the SQL syntax is not checked when the expression is COMMITed but is later validated when the CASE generators tries to incorporate it as part of an SQL statement.

User Help Text—context-sensitive help for the end user. Adding user help text at the column, table, or module level means that a separate help form with its context sensitive information is made accessible. For more on this table-driven help system see Section 5.7 below.

Where/Validation Condition—an SQL condition. When it's entered for a table on the *Module Data Usage (detailed) Screen* (see section 5.3), it restricts the rows displayed (just as it would in the SQL*Forms Designer on the *Block Definition Screen* in the field "Default Where/Order by"). The "Where/Validation Condition" also provides the possibility of defining one check constraint on data entry for each column. Triggers are created by the CASE generators based on these definitions.

Screens on which Edit Text is available are:

> *Table Definition*
>
> *Column Definition*
>
> *Column Derivation and Validation*
>
> *Table Key Constraints Definition*–for primary, unique, foreign key, and check constraint
>
> *Module Definition*
>
> *Module Data Usage (detailed)*–for table and column usage

Are all options available from all of these screens?

> No. Of the five categories mentioned above only **Description** and **Notes** are available from all of these screens. **User Help Text** can be defined on all but the *Table Key Constraints Definition Screen*. The **Derivation Expression** is always associated to a column's definition, validation, and usage. The **Where Condition** is defined on the *Module Data Usage Screen*, and **Validation** can be entered for check constraints on the *Table Key Constraints Definition Screen*, page 2, as well as on the *Column Definition* and *Column Validation and Derivation* screens.

4.9   Key Constraints—Referential Integrity

Before implementing the indexes for our tables, we need to validate all of the keys as well as to determine referential integrity rules for foreign keys. We use the *Table Key Constraints Definition Screen* (see Fig. 4.10) under the *Table Columns and Keys Menu* to perform these functions. There is also a hot key [Block Menu] available from the *Table Definition Screen* for directly accessing this screen. We begin by carrying out a last check of our UID's and candidate keys on page one, where we can scroll through all existing unique key definitions. We can also enter user-friendly error messages for each key. On this page is an unusual option: an "updatable" primary key ("U" field after "Primary Key Name"). Relational theory doesn't support this feature, but Oracle offers it because of occasional business requirements.

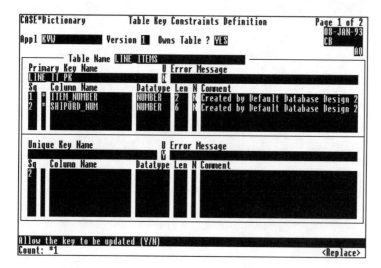

Figure 4.10
Table Key Constraints
Definition Screen—
Page 1

On page two we begin defining delete, update, and transferability rules for foreign keys. We can also define check constraints here (see Fig. 4.11). A quick way to determine which tables have foreign keys is to look at the latest ERD (see Appendix D) and check all tables based on entities adjoining "crow's foot" relationship ends. The transferability field requires a "Y"es or "N"o response to the question: "can this foreign key be updated?" (i.e., "can this relationship be transferred to another occurrence after creation?"). Typically the answer is "Y" for foreign keys belonging to reference tables (allowed types, classes, etc.) and "N" when the foreign key is part of the primary key, which is not normally updatable (e.g., shipping-order number from LINE_ITEMS table).

Figure 4.11
Table Key Constraints
Definition Screen—
Page 2

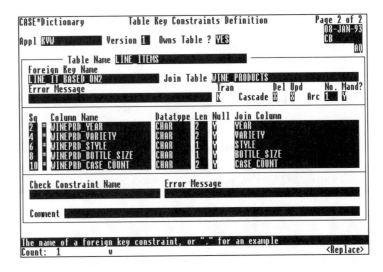

Our next concern is rules for deletion. Here we decide what should happen to detail rows when we attempt to delete a master row:

C—cascade deletion: if a master has existing detail rows, they should be deleted when the master is, as with the line-item details of a shipping order.

X—restricted: a master should not be deleted if it has existing detail rows; for example, an account type should not be deleted as long as it is used by existing accounts.

N—nullify: if the master is deleted, the foreign key in its associated detail rows should be set to NULL, as, for example, when a department is eliminated and the rows identifying equipment belonging to it have their foreign keys nullified until they have a new owner.

D—default: set the foreign keys to their default value if the master is deleted; the default value is defined in the *Column Definition Screen* and the value entered there MUST match an existing master record. For example, when a warehouse is no longer used by KVW, foreign keys of inventory item rows associated with that warehouse are changed to their default value: the main warehouse at the winery.

Referential integrity as related to the update rule (entered in the field "Cascade Upd" on page two) only applies to those master tables with an updatable primary key. Again, each master table must be defined as updatable on page one before update rules can be applied to corresponding foreign keys. Our selection at this field is always "X", because we have not defined any primary keys as updatable.

These tasks are not something we rush through in our workshop. Decisions concerning referential integrity determine the most fundamental structure of our database and provide an excellent opportunity to check our design. Properly understanding data relationships and how they reflect business rules can make the difference between a highly reliable and a poor information system.

4.10   On Indexes

If our aim is to design a database for high performance, it's very important to understand how indexes work—how they are used and should be used. Tuning a database and applications is such an important issue that it deserves its own book. So here we limit our description to how indexes work and how we use them in our workshop.

ORACLE V6 uses the "B-Tree" method of indexing, which is the most common for relational databases. ORACLE7 offers a choice between B-Tree and Hashing. The B-Tree is a multi-level system where "non-dense" indexes at the top levels reference pages of the next index down, creating a pyramid-like structure. Typically, three layers of indexes are used (except for very large tables), the bottom level, of course, containing the data and pointers to the actual row addresses. ORACLE V6 provides two views, INDEX_STATS and INDEX_HISTOGRAM, which are populated when an index is VALIDATEd. The height of an index (its number of layers), selectivity of keys, and space usage are among the data supplied by these views.

We've already checked all our keys and can now proceed to the *Data Design Utilities Menu*. Here we run the *Default Index Design Utility* that generates our index definitions.

It should be clarified that all the work we've done so far regarding tables, columns, sequences, and indexes during the design stage has been on the level of definition, not creation. No actual tables exist yet, but after we've checked and refined the results of this utility we will be able to begin creating the database for our workshop.

Now we move to the *Index Definition Screen* (see Fig. 4.12) under the *Database Design Menu*. Here we verify that all indexes we need have been defined for primary and foreign keys. We also may need to delete some indexes for small tables where a full table scan would provide better performance. In our workshop, we add only one item to our index definitions: KVWTABS will be their tablespace. It's also possible to use separate tablespaces for indexes and data, and by storing them on different physical disks some contention problems can be avoided. Other options available on this screen are physical storage allocation parameters, allocation of free space for index growth, and other settings that a DBA uses in deciding how to implement the indexes.

Figure 4.12
Index Definition Screen

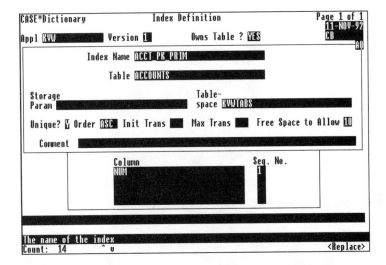

4.11   Additional Design Issues

We now devote a little time to subjects not normally included in a workshop, but which can be of importance during a larger-scale design stage.

The screens under the *Distributed Capability Menu* (see Fig. 4.13) are used to record information for developing distributed databases. They are built on extensions to CASE*Dictionary that comprise a facility called "User Extensibility" (see Appendix A). Some of the new objects available are "Node", "Installation", and "Location". These are used in association with standard CASE elements. For example, the *Distributed Database Definition Screen* is based on a node-to-table association, while the *Distributed Processing Definition Screen* relates nodes to modules. Frequency and required response time are two of the attributes associated with modules on a node. For tables, volumetric information is stored as well as whether or not a table is replicated, that is, duplicated on another node. These screens, together with the *Business Unit Use of Node Definition Screen*, and the *Network Connection Definition Screen,* (based on a node-to-node association), are tools for storing information about the network design.

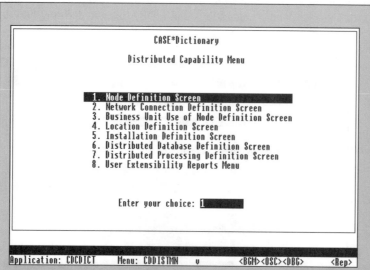

Figure 4.13
Distributed Capability
Menu

The *DBA Options Menu* (see Fig. 4.14) provides an interface for ORACLE DBAs either to document an existing ORACLE RDBMS (including operating systems files and storage definitions) or to enter those specifications through these screens and use the DDL Generator to create a command file (CDCDDL. SQL). This file can be executed where and when the DBA wants to create an ORACLE database, rollback segments, and/or table-spaces. To optimize the physical implementation of the database, storage clauses (for example, for tables and tablespaces) can be defined. Helpful information including an estimated size of the database is provided by the *Database/Index Sizing Utility* based on volumetric figures entered for each table. The command file can also be used to establish access to the database by defining ORACLE users. Besides the general access rights to the database, most users will require access rights to database objects such as tables or views. The *Database Object Access Definition Screen* can be called from the *Database User Definition Screen* as well as from the *View Definition* and the *Table Definition Screens*. To limit the space that users can occupy, quotas are given within a particular tablespace. If this is not established, the user has unlimited possibilities to "hog the disk." ORACLE users can also be members of one or more groups that are defined to control access to a particular module. Security is a major issue in any production system but is not a factor in our workshop.

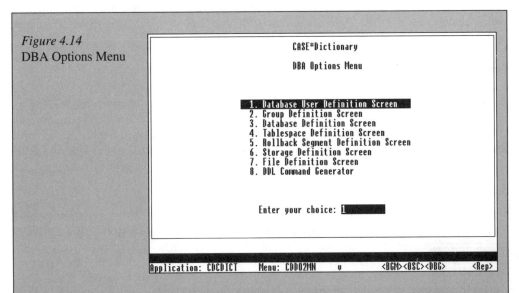

Figure 4.14
DBA Options Menu

Besides the database, application (see next chapter), and network design, these are other areas to cover before a complete system design is achieved:

- audit and control procedures

- back-up and recovery plans

- a completed system test plan

- drafts of documentation

- a design for the transition stage (including hardware and software installation, data take-on, support facilities, user training, and user acceptance)

Again, these activities are beyond the scope of a normal workshop and are more suitable for consulting projects.

4.12   Creating a Relational Database with the DDL Command Generator

As we mentioned at the beginning of this chapter, our method in a workshop is to create the database before designing application modules. From the CASE*Method point of view, we're temporarily leaving the design stage and beginning implementation. We do this essentially because our clients tend to prefer it.

The *DDL* (Data Definition Language) *Command Generator* is accessible from several different submenus in CASE*Dictionary. This utility uses existing definitions for a variety of different object types selected by the user, creates a script "CDCDDL.SQL", and offers to execute the script to create "live" objects. The broadest scopes of object types are "DBA" and "USER", which include, under DBA: Database, Grant, Rollback Segment, and Tablespace; and under USER: Cluster, Index, Sequence, Table, and View. A single object type can also be selected from this list, generating a script that implements that object alone. Conversely, the use of wild cards permits the creation of groups of objects.

Before our "USER" objects can be implemented, we need to create the tablespace KVWTABS by running the *DDL Command Generator* for the "TS" object type. This is required because we've declared that tablespace for all our tables and indexes. To run the generator in this mode requires DBA privileges. A quick way to change the log-on for this (or any other) purpose is to use the [Redefine User Name/Password] key (which is dependent on the Oracle*Terminal definition).

Once KVWTABS has been created, we run the *DDL Command Generator* again, this time entering "USER" at the object type prompt (see Fig. 4.15). We then ask for "Comments" to be inserted for our columns and enter "Y"es to have constraints created for the tables (for example, primary key, foreign key, and check constraints). Finally we ask for verification. This provides an on-screen overview listing of the selected user objects before the actual creation of the SQL script.

```
*********************************************************************
* CASE*Dictionary Utilities - DDL Command Generator
*
* - Use  '%'  and  '_'  wild cards for string searches on objects
* e.g  %DEM, %, DEM_RT% etc
*********************************************************************

Enter Application System Name (. to stop) : KVW >

Enter Version number                  : 1 >

Enter Database type (ORACLE/DB2) : ORACLE >


Enter Database Object type (? help/. end) : > user

Do you want comments inserted for columns (Y/N) : N > y

Do you want constraints created for tables (Y/N) : N > y

Input session complete. Do you want verification (Y/N) : Y >
```

Figure 4.15
DDL Command
Generator

The default name for this script, CDCDDL.SQL, can be changed, but doing so means that the script can no longer be run by the *DDL Command Generator*. Instead, it would have to be executed from SQL*Plus (or SQL*DBA). We choose to let the generator do the work and accept the default script name. Of course, this script can also be run on another computer if the database is to be implemented there.

And with the press of a button, our new database is actually born!

4.13   Implementing Reference Tables

Now we make our first foray into the CASE generators world by turning to the *CASE*Generator for Reference Tables Screen* (see Fig. 4.16) under the *CASE*Generator Utilities Menu.* Here we can load:

1. user help text,

2. valid values and range checks, and

3. code control sequence definitions

into reference tables for our applications. We work with these tools at this point in our workshop because they all deal with data, while the other CASE generators implement modules. On the other hand, if we add user help text while creating modules, we'll need to run this utility again.

Figure 4.16
CASE*Generator for
Reference Tables Screen

```
CASE*Generator        CASE*Generator for Reference Tables        Page 1 of 1
                                                                  08-JAN-93
Appl KVW          Version 1                                       CB
                                                                     A0

 Update help tables

        Module name     :
        Table name      :

 Update reference code tables

        Table name      : %

 Update code control tables

        Sequence name   :

   To invoke utility; enter relevant utility block and select [Commit] key




Reference values will be entered for this table; wildcards accepted
Count: *0                                              <List><Replace>
```

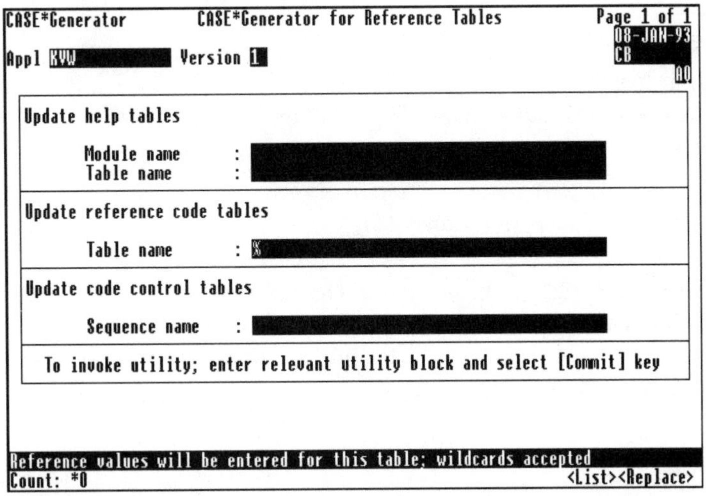

We begin with the user help text that's been defined at the table and column level. In the "Update help tables" block we leave the "Module name" field blank since we haven't designed our processes yet. Then we enter "%" (wild card: select all) after "Table name" and press COMMIT. A utility begins that loads our definitions into the CASE*Dictionary table CG_FORM_HELP. On the first run, this table doesn't exist so we enter "Y" during the dialogue to have it created. We then select KVWTABS as the location for the new table.

Next we load all valid values and range checks from attribute, domain, and column definitions into the table CG_REF_CODES through the "Update reference code tables" block by following the same steps as in the first block.

If we were not using ORACLE's sequence numbers and had entered "Y" under "Code control" in the *Sequence Definition Screen*, we could now load these definitions into the table CG_CODES_CONTROL by COMMITting with the cursor in the "Update code control tables" block. CASE*Generator for SQL*Forms would later add accessible code for sequence incrementation. Using this method eliminates gaps in sequences but doesn't provide for caching, besides being a fundamentally slower and more complex operation than sequencing. In a busy multi-user environment these factors could cause contention and general performance problems.

Without any change of the user preferences HPTABL (scope of help text table), DVTABL (scope of reference codes table), and CCTABL (scope of code controls table), we define these tables systemwide, but their scope can be limited to one application. Then we need to create synonyms to point correctly to CG_FORM_HELP, CG_REF_CODES, and CG_CODES_CONTROL. It's important to know the names of these tables because they have to be sent with the application if it's moved to a different machine for production. This is also why we keep them in the same tablespace (KVWTABS) as the application.

The ability to manage tables separately from applications makes these utilities very powerful. If a change is needed in any definition of values contained in one of the tables, it's first specified in CASE*Dictionary. Then the appropriate utility is simply re-executed, causing the change to be immediately incorporated into all running applications that use that table.

4.14   So Where Are We?

Well, we're right in the thick of it! Our database has been designed and implemented and we're about to turn our function specifications into application modules. Unless we keep our heads up, we risk drowning in an ocean of details. (See the following box for ways to handle some of the fish in that ocean.)

At this point we often hear the question, "What do I need to do if my data structure changes—if I find new attributes and entities while having 'live' tables out there?" Here's one answer:

To enter a few attributes:

1. Enter the attributes on the *Attribute Definition Screen*.

2. Enter the equivalent columns on the *Column Definition Screen*.

3. Run the *Alter Database Command Generator* from the *Reconciliation Menu*. This utility cross-checks the definitions stored in CASE*Dictionary against the ones in the on-line data dictionary and generates ALTER TABLE statements. The script that's created, CDRK.SQL, can be edited and when it's executed your "live" database changes.

To enter new entities:

1. Enter the new entities via the Entity Diagrammer or directly into CASE*Dictionary.

2. Add attributes and all required details.

3. Create table definitions via the *Fastpath Table Mapping Screen*.

4. Run the *DDL Command Generator* selecting "T" (table) as the object, then mentioning not only the new tables, but all the ones to which new relationships exist, so that the proper foreign keys can be created. We recommend looking at and possibly editing this script (CDCDDL.SQL) before executing it.

Sophisticated tools allow us to analyze information needs in depth, but require intelligence and discrimination to produce high-quality results. One of our team members says that the workshop environment, in which broadly drawn models are so quickly transformed into specific design elements, has forced her to see what a complex process application development really is. She wonders whatever made her think she could do it properly without the kinds of structured methods CASE provides. It's a good question.

5

Application Design and Implementation

With our database in place, we now begin the task of designing and generating application modules. Running the CASE generators brings a moment of truth regarding much detailed work already done defining functions, their connections to business units, and their entity usages (CRUD—see Section 3.12). If our cross-checking of elementary functions, entities, and attributes has been thorough and accurate, then our module design will be equally good. And whether we're creating screens, reports, or menus, it's time to enter the complex and powerful world of user preferences, which greatly influences the layout and behavior of our application.

5.1   Creating Module Definitions

The first step in module design is very straightforward: we simply run the *Default Module Specification Utility* under the *Module Design Utilities Menu*. This activates the *Default Application Designer* (DAD), which generates first-cut definitions for *candidate* modules —those that we can later accept or delete. It uses analysis specifications already in CASE*Dictionary to decide whether an elementary function should be turned into a report, screen, utility, or manual procedure. So how is this magic accomplished?

One major data source for the DAD is our function/entity matrix (see Fig. 3.13). During analysis we established CRUD usages between entities and elementary functions. If the DAD finds that a function only retrieves data from entities, it looks at the "Response Needed" parameter from the function definition. If we entered IMMEDIATE here, it determines that the function should be implemented as a screen; otherwise, it will be implemented as a report. If "Create", "Update", "Delete", or "Archive" usages were defined for a function in relation to any entity, DAD again references the "Response" parameter. If IMMEDIATE was selected (or if it was left blank), DAD sets the module type to SCREEN. If OVERNIGHT was chosen, it recommends a utility. The usage "Other" doesn't seem to influence these decisions. If DAD cannot logically determine a module type, it suggests a screen by default. This rather complex process is graphically described in our matrix, Figure 5.1.

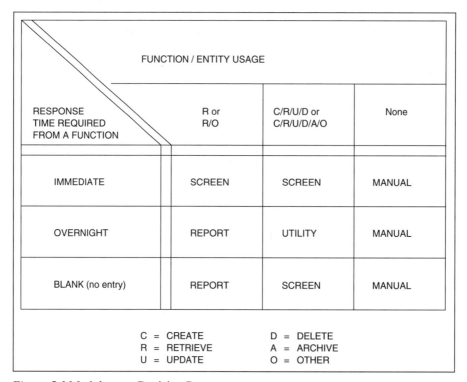

RESPONSE TIME REQUIRED FROM A FUNCTION	R or R/O	C/R/U/D or C/R/U/D/A/O	None
IMMEDIATE	SCREEN	SCREEN	MANUAL
OVERNIGHT	REPORT	UTILITY	MANUAL
BLANK (no entry)	REPORT	SCREEN	MANUAL

FUNCTION / ENTITY USAGE

C = CREATE   D = DELETE
R = RETRIEVE   A = ARCHIVE
U = UPDATE   O = OTHER

Figure 5.1 Module-type Decision Process

But the *Default Application Designer* can make other decisions about elementary functions. For example, if no entity usages have been defined for a function, DAD flags it to be implemented as a manual module. And if we've set the user preference INCMAN to "N"o (don't include manual modules), no modules will be defined for those functions in CASE*Dictionary. The default "Y"es causes manual procedures to be included, which can be a useful way to ensure that they're taken into account regarding security requirements.

Another circumstance under which a function could fail to be turned into a module is when two functions within the same business unit have identical entity usages and the user preference MERGEL is set to "Y"es, which is the default. In this case, DAD merges the two functions into one module. If this is not desirable, it is easy to use the *Copy Module Screen* to duplicate it.

It is also possible to limit the scope of the system being created in relation to a given function hierarchy. This is accomplished with the user preference TOPFUN, which establishes the highest level function to be processed by DAD. When TOPFUN is associated with a particular function label, DAD defines modules based on all elementary functions below it in the hierarchy. Of course, our workshop application is small enough not to require this preference.

With a procedure similar to the one for creating table definitions, we're now about to confirm a first-cut module design. From the *Default Module Specification Utility*, which has already run the DAD and generated candidate module definitions, we proceed to the *Candidate Module Specification Acceptance Screen* (see Fig. 5.2). Here we delete candidate modules that we don't want. Only when we're finished editing this list do we COMMIT our selection to CASE*Dictionary.

An interesting note: one of our workshop participants discovered by accident that the DAD cannot be run twice for the same module. As soon as it finds short names or module names that already exist (either on the *Module Definition Screen* or the *Candidate Module Specification Acceptance Screen*), it aborts. Sometimes using TOPFUN can allow us to avoid this problem, since we can specify a single new function or group of functions to be defined as modules.

Figure 5.2
Candidate Module
Specification Acceptance
Screen

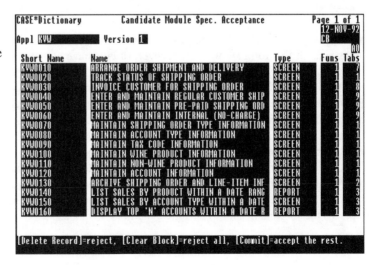

5.2   Refining Module Definitions

Under the *Module Control Menu* (see Fig. 5.3) are several screens that can contribute project control information for application development. During a larger-scale CASE project, we would first recommend the *Module Planning Screen* for storing information on assigning modules to particular projects and tasks. Time estimates according to the complexity of a module can also be entered. Of course a workshop doesn't require this much organization, and we do little more with this screen than point out its value for our participants' future use. Oracle is developing an integrated graphical project control package that is much more sophisticated than these screens.

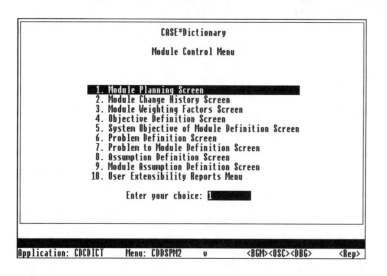

Figure 5.3
Module Control Menu

We move on to the *Module Definition Screen*, where we begin to refine our first-cut design. A quick scan of this form shows us that several fields have already been filled by the DAD (see Fig. 5.4). The "Short Name" has been automatically generated as a composite of the application name and a four-digit number that is incremented by ten for each successive module. Besides being used as the operating system file name, it also becomes the default screen or report name (depending on its type) that appears on pull-down menus. Since we've named our functions descriptively ("SA_MTNACCT", etc.), we decide to replace the system-generated short name with one of our own. Next comes "Module Name", which was taken from our function description and acts as the default for the top title on screens and reports. It is also used as the default name on full-screen menus. However, whatever is entered in the "Titles" section of this screen overrides the defaults both of module name and short name: "Short Title" replaces the short name and "Top Title", the module name.

Figure 5.4
Module Definition Screen

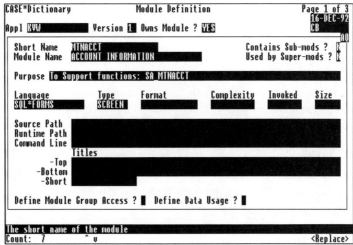

```
CASE*Dictionary                 Module Definition         Page 1 of 3
                                                          16-DEC-92
Appl KVW          Version 1 Owns Module ? YES             CB
                                                          00
    Short Name  MTNACCT                     Contains Sub-mods ? [
    Module Name ACCOUNT INFORMATION         Used by Super-mods ? [

    Purpose To Support functions: SA MTNACCT

    Language           Type     Format      Complexity  Invoked   Size
    SQL*FORMS          SCREEN

    Source Path
    Runtime Path
    Command Line
                 Titles
           -Top
        -Bottom
         -Short

    Define Module Group Access ? ▮  Define Data Usage ? ▮

The short name of the module
Count:  7          ^  v                                    <Replace>
```

Another important part of our module definition is the "Language" and "Type" relationship. As mentioned above, DAD has decided on a type for each module that corresponds to a specific module generation language. We can change that language by selecting from a list of values. For example, DAD (guided by user preferences) chooses SQL*Forms as the language to be used for a "SCREEN" module. If we select SQL*ReportWriter instead, the "Type" field is automatically changed from SCREEN to REPORT. In other words, it's easy to correct the *Default Application Designer*'s module-type selection here.

The module definitions indirectly provide a quality check of our function definitions and their association with entities. Did we enter the desired RESPONSE time? Is our CRUD usage correct? In fact, we refer to DAD as a "sanity check" on our workshop analysis.

The default value for the field "Format" is "MASTER/DETAIL". This will be used by CASE*Generator for SQL*Forms to build referential integrity into the forms.

Defaults for the fields "Source Path", "Run time Path", and "Command Line" are taken from the *Module Language Definition Screen*. The command line, for example

    iap <MODULE> <UN>/<PW>

is a SQL*Menu command line where the text "<MODULE>" is replaced by the runtime path. This command is used when a form is run from a SQL*Menu menu. Then <UN>/<PW> is substituted for the current username/password (so that it doesn't have to be reentered).

Using the [Edit Text] key on the *Module Definition Screen* allows entry of User Help Text. This information will be made available at the highest (module) level (see Sections 4.8 and 5.7 for more on Edit Text and User Help Text).

5.3   Detailed Data Usage of Modules

Now it's time to define table and column usages in more detail by selecting the *Module Data Usage (detailed) Screen* (MDU(detailed)) from the *Module Design Menu* (see Fig. 5.5). Whatever we do here will directly influence the generation of forms and reports. The *MDU(detailed) Screen* should not be confused with the *Module Data Usage Screen*, which is used for impact analysis. The *Default Application Designer* has already filled in much information on the *MDU(detailed) Screen*, both on the table and column level. For the most part, DAD has forwarded the data from pages three and four of the *Column Definition Screen*.

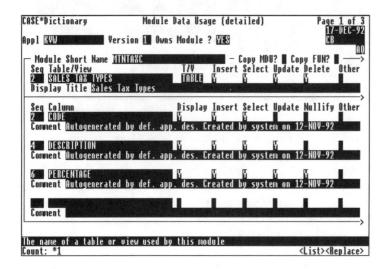

Figure 5.5
Module Data Usage
(detailed) Screen—
Page 1

The first block is called the "Detailed Table Usage" (DTU) and displays the table usages for a given module based on our function/entity matrix. We now have an additional chance to examine these and correct them if necessary. We also notice that the tables have been ordered by DAD and given sequence numbers. These may need to be resequenced before they can be properly linked (see Section 5.5 for more on this). Clearly, we already need to have a fairly detailed idea of our form's layout (based on user input) by this time.

Beneath the DTU is another larger block called the "Detailed Column Usage" (DCU). The five columns that on the DTU represent CRUD usages for tables seem to extend down into the DCU, but they actually have a rather different meaning in the second block. DAD automatically fills the "Insert", "Select", and "Update" columns in the DCU based on the entry into the table-level columns above them. However, the DCU "Insert" column has nothing to do with adding new records, as it does on the table level. Instead, it flags a particular field in the module as being either enterable for a cursor or not. This can cause problems if, for example, the table being referenced in the DTU has a "query only" usage ("Select" = "Y", all other usages blank). In such a case, DAD essentially decides that none of the fields holding column values can be entered. However, SQL*Forms requires that every block have one enterable field. So one of our tasks is to refine the column usages for query-only blocks. Alternatively, an

"Update" usage at the DTU level would be transferred to all columns beneath it, including primary keys. This could be a problem, but see below how the generator resolves it.

Another point to consider is that DAD enters "Y" or blank into the "Nullify" attribute based on whether or not the column value is defined as "required" in the column definition (a required field cannot be NULL). One of our team members also made a useful discovery when he mistakenly set the "Display" attribute to "N" (blanking the field has the same effect). This not only blanks out all the other column usages but also deletes field definition details on pages two and three for that row (once the entry is COMMITted). Fortunately, by deleting the DCU record, then re-inserting it, the three pages of data for that record are restored (otherwise we'd need to re-enter it manually).

Page two of the *MDU(detailed) Screen* contains detailed column definition data regarding display types, formats, prompts, and hint text (see Fig. 5.6). Again, what is entered here will be used directly by the CASE generators. A common warning issued by the generator regards display length, found on this page. When using a NUMBER format for a column with decimal places, the length must be increased by two beyond the number of digits, one for a plus/minus sign and one for the decimal place. RMONEY format lengths must only be increased by one. Though the generator may still issue warnings, these fields will then function properly. Of course, we could anticipate this and increase the display lengths of all such columns on the *Column Definition Screen* (see Section 4.6), which would be preferable, since they would then be defined correctly for all modules.

Figure 5.6
Module Data Usage
(detailed) Screen—
Page 2

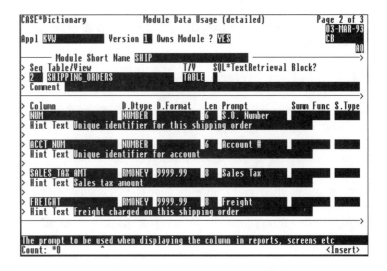

Page three primarily has to do with creating reports, so we return to it when we begin working with report modules (see Section 5.12, Fig. 5.30).

In our workshop we've started studying the *MDU(detailed) Screen* in the context of our simplest form modules: those that maintain reference and validation tables. This way we can more easily begin penetrating the complexities of the CASE generators. Once we're satisfied with data usages and field attributes for one of these modules, we go directly to the *CASE*Generator for SQL*Forms Generate Screen* (see Fig. 5.14) and generate our first form. This is a procedure we'll be repeating very often in our project, but this time we do it using all the system default settings, just to observe the process. The generator produces the simple reference table maintenance form we wanted without a hitch (see Fig. 5.7), but our participants immediately notice something: the default date format in the top right-hand corner (Dy,DD-Mon). Our client doesn't use this format, so we've got our first opportunity to investigate the new world of user preferences.

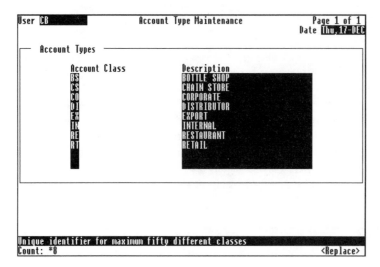

Figure 5.7
Account Type
Maintenance Form

5.4   On User Preferences

Before we jump in and simply change the user preference for our screen date format, an introduction to the extensive subject that lies behind this action will prove useful. User preferences are settings that provide the CASE generators with a wide variety of instructions on how to present forms, reports, and the information contained in them. These settings allow an application's look and feel to be precisely defined; once those defined conventions are agreed upon, they can also be enforced for all work done on that application.

During our first form generation we accepted the default set of user preferences that came with the product. This worked for us, but sometimes one or two of those settings need to be changed before the generator can be run. For example, if the hardware platform on which CASE has been installed is different from the terminals being used for development, the user preference DFTCRT (Default Terminal Definition) has to be reset to match those terminals. Another common initial obstacle involves the user preference HLPFRM (Help Form). In this case, depending both on the hardware platform being used and the software release, the default path to the Help Form might be incorrectly set (enter "cgen20" in the path-name instead of "cgen"). In the OS/2 environment of our workshop, however, it works fine.

Figure 5.8
User Preferences Screen
for SQL*Forms—Page 1

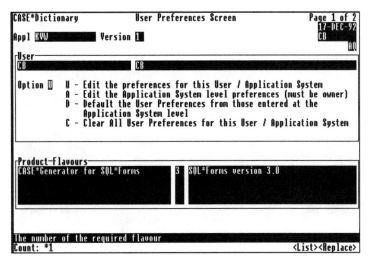

The *User Preferences Screen* for SQL*Forms (see Fig. 5.8) is found under the *CASE*Generator for SQL*Forms Menu*. One of the first things we notice on this form is the distinction made between "User" and "Application" system levels. The Application set of preferences is what it sounds like: it is intended to be used by everyone working on a given application. The User set is for an individual user. Our preferences can be edited on both these levels, but if we generate for the first time and have already set preferences both at the Application and User levels, the generator will apply the User-level set. This is a general principle with Oracle: the more specific overrides the more global ("User" overrides "Application").

So what is a preference set? It's an overlay of the Default set. As this implies, we cannot use the User and Application sets together. But we can forward the Application settings to the User level by entering "D" in the "Option" field on page one of the *User Preferences Screen*. So these are the sets we have discovered so far:

DEFAULT

DEFAULT + USER

DEFAULT + APPLICATION

The "C" option does reset the User-level set to default values, but it doesn't do this for the Application set. There's actually no automatic means of resetting Application-level preferences.

Once we've settled on the settings for this first page we press [Next Block] twice (from the "Product Flavours" block) to access a pop-up window on page two from which we can select the user preferences we want to edit or view (see Fig. 5.9). These entry options are as follows:

Name: Specific user preference and/or wild cards.

Type: A search mechanism that accepts wild cards and brings a range of user preferences (i.e. LAYOUT%).

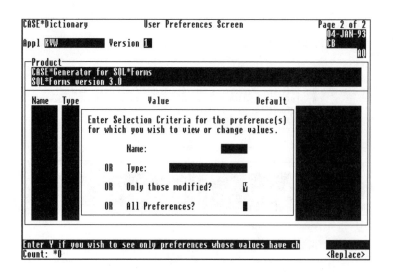

Figure 5.9
User Preference Screen
with Pop-up Window

Only those modified? This is especially useful to view the edited set of the level we're working on. It's also the only (fairly) quick way to change the Application-level set back to default, though we still need to type the default values back in.

All Preferences? This is good for familiarizing ourselves with the options available for this product.

We recommend using the list of values where available, as well as the context-sensitive help (press [Help]), which people in our workshops especially like (see Fig. 5.10), first because it allows them to avoid poring over manuals and also because it points at dependencies between preferences. For example, some user preferences are toggles that switch other preferences on or off, as with BSTUBS (block stubs), which does this with BLKIND (block indentation). Other preferences like SAVPRF (save preferences) influence the generation process of a form. If we leave SAVPRF at its default "Y", then whenever we generate, our settings are saved with the module.

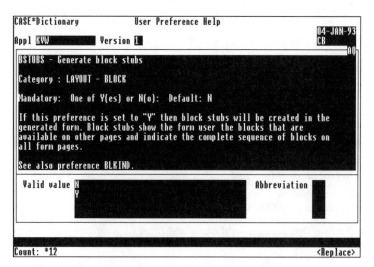

Figure 5.10
User Preference Help

Now we proceed again to the *CASE*Generator for SQL*Forms Generate Screen* (see Fig. 5.14) where we can examine it in more detail. One of our options here is whether or not to use saved preferences. If the field "Use saved preferences?" is left blank and we've changed some preferences, then the dialog during the generator run asks us which set we want to use—the one previously saved or the current one (see Fig. 5.20). If "N" has been entered here, it doesn't ask and uses the current values. But if it finds "Y", the dialog doesn't ask us and uses the previously saved values.

Another option is "Override preferences?". Normally this is set to "N", but if it is changed to "Y" we can add to whichever set is active during the generator dialog. This is then included in the saved set for the module being generated if SAVPRF = "Y".

A complete list of user preference settings follows:

> DEFAULT
>
> DEFAULT + USER SET
>
> DEFAULT + APPLICATION SET
>
> DEFAULT + SAVED SET (from the last generation)
>
> DEFAULT + OVERRIDE
>
> DEFAULT + USER SET + OVERRIDE
>
> DEFAULT + APPLICATION SET + OVERRIDE
>
> DEFAULT + SAVED SET + OVERRIDE

We hope that specifying these combinations of preference sets helps clarify how they work. Figure 5.11 summarizes the decision making process.

So with a necessarily brief introduction to a very large subject, we are ready to accommodate our client's date-format convention by changing the Application-level user preference PHDMSK (Page Header Date Mask) to MM/DD/YY.

During a workshop, every participant examines the options available by generating with different User sets. In a real-life situation, the same could be done during a prototyping phase. But when the building of production applications starts, the project team should agree on one set of preferences, establish them at the Application level, and discourage the use of Override and User-level preferences. Only in this way can a uniform look and feel be achieved throughout a team-built application.

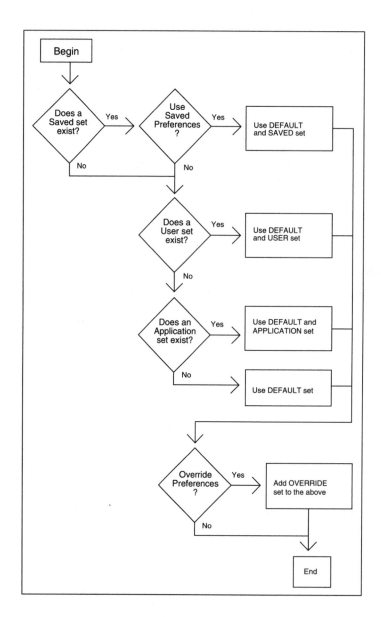

Figure 5.11
Selection of User
Preference Sets

5.5   Specifying Links

Seeing all the tables associated with a module on the *MDU(detailed) Screen* might cause us to assume that they're already linked (or JOINed) together, but this would be a mistake. To link tables together for a module, there are two possible methods: either we do it beforehand by using the *Linking between Detailed Table Usages Screen*, or we respond to the generator's dialog at run time.

On the *CASE* Generator for SQL*Forms Generate Screen* (see Fig. 5.14), there's a field with the prompt: "Define links between table usages?". If we enter "Y" here, the *Linking between*

Detailed Table Usages Screen appears (see Fig. 5.12). It displays the same list of tables we saw on the *MDU(detailed) Screen* (see Section 5.3 above). If we still don't like the order of tables, we can change it on this screen. To do this, though, it's important to remember: COMMIT changed sequence numbers *before* establishing the links (see below).

Figure 5.12
Linking between
Detailed Table Usages

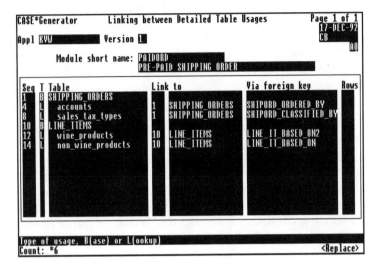

We are now actually engaged in designing the overall structure of our form. To do this, three questions have to be considered:

- Which tables are used as bases for blocks?

- In which order should these tables be sequenced?

- Which details from nonbase (or look-up) tables are required?

Since links can only be established via existing foreign keys, we begin by studying our ERD and deciding on a master base table for the module in question. When we enter our design onto the *Linking between DTU Screen*, here's how the tables should be ordered:

1. Base table—first block

2. Look-up tables for this block—depending on the order of columns in the DCU

3. Base table—second block, etc.

Next we fill in the second column ("T"), indicating whether a record is for a base or look-up table. Note how the names of look-ups are indented and switched to lower-case, making them easier to distinguish.

The "Link" column, though, is the key to this screen. Here we use the sequence numbers we've entered actually to flag the links. "Link" numbers must always be lower than the sequence number of the table being linked, so defining the correct order of tables was necessary preparation for this step. When we enter the "Link" number, its related table and foreign key names are automatically filled in. Fig. 5.12 is an example of a typical master/ detail form.

Sometimes we might want to display information from a look-up table that has no direct foreign key relationship to a block's base table. In this case we list any intermediate look-up tables in order of their relationships to the base table and to one another until we reach the look-up table we actually want, linking them together in a sort of chain. These "in-between" tables need to be listed on the *MDU(detailed) Screen*, but can be completely nondisplayed, containing only the relevant primary and foreign key columns. Thus we obey the two basic linking rules presented above:

1. Links can only be established via existing foreign keys.

2. "Link" numbers must always be lower than the sequence number of the table being linked.

Again, we could leave the *Linking between DTU Screen* blank and let CASE*Generator for SQL*Forms prompt us at run time for potential links (see Fig. 5.13). It asks us about linking tables that contain descriptors (such as "Name" and "Description" fields, which we defined in the *Column Definition Screen*) and have foreign key relationships to our base table, even if they're not on the *MDU(detailed) Screen*. This is called *inferred* or *implicit* linking. But using the *Linking between DTU Screen* provides an excellent overview of table relationships and is a good exercise for planning a form, so we strongly recommend going through it before generation.

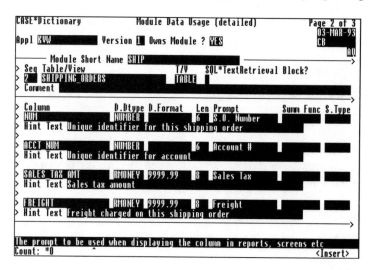

Figure 5.13
CASE*Generator for
SQL*Forms
Linking Dialog

There is an additional form type that cannot really be handled by the *Linking between DTU Screen*. This is the matrix form, where the base table of a detail block actually needs to be linked to two master tables (which the linking screen currently cannot do). We actually specify this form as a "MATRIX" in the "Format" field on the *Module Definition Screen*. For this type of form, the right approach is to use the *Linking between DTU Screen* to link the detail table to the **first** master. Then, during the generation dialog, when *CASE*Generator for SQL*Forms* asks if we want to link the second master, we simply enter "Y"es, establishing the complete matrix link.

5.6   CASE*Generator for SQL*Forms

It is finally time to start the iterative process of generating forms. We've already discussed the *CASE*Generator for SQL*Forms Generate Screen* (see Fig. 5.14) with respect to user preferences (see Section 5.3 above). Now we start exploring the generation process itself, with its run-time parameters and dialog. For an experienced user, forms generation can be a very simple procedure. But this is only because all the wrinkles have been worked out beforehand. We know enough to check detailed table and column usages thoroughly for inconsistencies. We know about making sure that certain number fields have long enough display lengths to prevent unhappy comments from the dialog. But the best way to begin learning how to anticipate problems, of course, is to run the generator, and keep running it until it becomes thoroughly familiar.

Figure 5.14
CASE*Generator for
SQL*Forms Generate
Screen

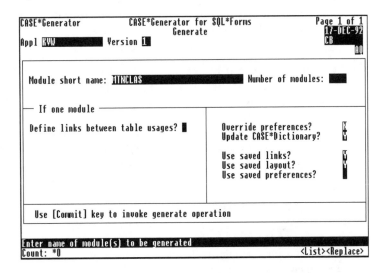

Going first to the *Generate Screen* itself, we see some entry fields we have not yet discussed:

Use saved links? If we accept the default "Y"es, the generator uses the explicitly defined links. Whenever it finds a new DTU for which we haven't explicitly defined a link, it asks us about it. If it finds "N"o, it queries us for each possible link.

Use saved layout? This is fairly straightforward. During generation we are queried regarding the number of base table rows we want to display in a block, provided that there's space for more than one. If we've already responded to this query once and we enter "Y"es here, the generator uses our last response for the next generation. Otherwise it calculates the available space again and asks us during the dialog.

Update CASE*Dictionary? This is also fairly clear: if the generator needs to make changes in usages or links during the run, should they be saved in CASE*Dictionary?

Now for the generation process itself. Lots of things can happen here, depending on what the generator finds in our database and module designs. We don't try to cover all the generator's warnings and error messages, but it is useful to mention some of the more common ones:

- The generator always notices inconsistencies in or between table and column usages. For example, if a primary key is non-updateable and we've forgotten to change the DCU by blanking out the "Update" field attribute, the generator will change it and issue a warning.

- If a primary key value is provided by a sequence, the generator makes sure that this column is non-enterable for the user, again sending a message.

- Now is the first time that derivation expressions and validation conditions are actually used as parts of SQL statements. Since there was no compilation before generation, this means we get our first error messages and warnings here if any of our Edit Text SQL entries are not correct.

- As mentioned before, if decimal places and plus/minus signs haven't been accounted for in the display lengths of column definitions or DCUs, we will be informed, but the layout is not changed. It also brings warnings in some cases where the field actually works anyway (see Section 5.3 above).

- In the beginning it is easy to forget that foreign keys in a base table should be displayed, rather than the primary keys of look-up tables. The generator is gentle here and just tells us the display usages on the look-up columns will be ignored.

These are some of the obstacles we run into most frequently during workshops. Anyone who uses the generators will soon add several more points to this list. As one last piece of advice, read and respond to the generator's dialog, don't respond and **then** read!

5.7   Further Examples

Here are some of the more common types of forms by using examples from our workshop. We've already seen a simple multi-row form in Figure 5.7. Now we can examine the implementation of context-sensitive user help text as we've applied it to this form. We mentioned in Section 4.8 that the Edit Text facility is used to enter the help text, on either a column, table, or module level (see Fig. 5.15). Our diagram shows us how the system determines which text to display as the user presses the [Help] key repeatedly. Text entered in the DCU block of the *MDU(detailed) Screen* is the first to be displayed. This overrides whatever has been entered on the *Column Definition Screen* (see Fig. 5.16), but if nothing was entered in the DCU, the column-level information is displayed. By pressing the [Help] key a second time, text entered on the DTU level, or, if none is there, from the *Table Definition Screen*, becomes visible. Another press on [Help] brings any text entered from the *Module Definition Screen*. Figure 5.17 shows how the column-level help text is displayed.

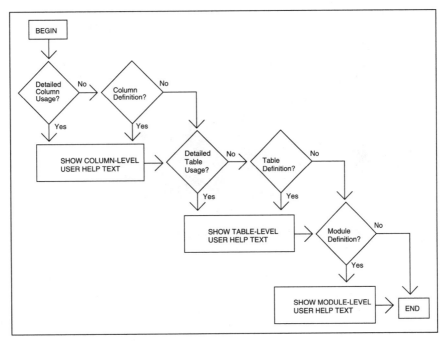

Figure 5.15 User Help Text—a Diagram on Entering and Displaying It

Figure 5.16
Input of User Help Text
on the Column
Definition Screen

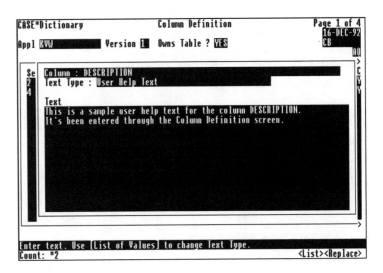

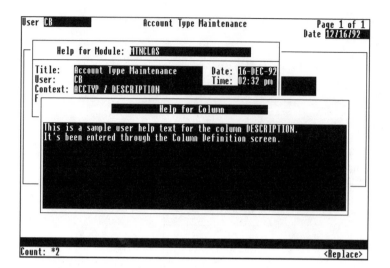

Figure 5.17
Display of User
Help Text

Figure 5.18 is an example of a single block form. This type can continue for several pages, all referring to the same block, and often contains lists of values (LOV) to look-up tables. Our example shows such an LOV for the account maintenance form, which is automatically derived from the existing foreign key relationship between the tables ACCOUNTS and ACCOUNT_TYPES. Alternatively, we could have used a reference code table to populate a list of valid values that we would define on the *Column Validation and Derivation Screen* or the *Domain Definition Screen*, then activate by running the *CASE*Generator for Reference Codes Utility*. However, when we implement validation via regular entities and tables, the user can maintain those tables. The second alternative requires that the developer do the maintenance work. That is, whenever a code or description changes, it has to be documented in CASE*Dictionary and the appropriate utility has to be run to update CG_REF_CODES. So this reference code table should only be used for relatively static validation data.

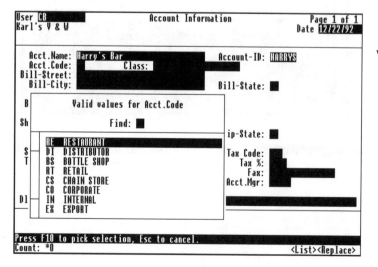

Figure 5.18
Account Information
with List of Valid Values

Figure 5.19
New Regular Customer
Order—a Master/Detail
Form

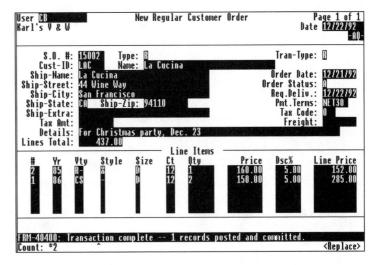

One of the central modules of our system is a typical master/detail form (Fig. 5.19). Its function is to handle entry of new shipping orders to be delivered to regular customers. We've used the SUM function on the MDU(detailed) Screen to provide a "Lines Total" field in the master block. The format of both blocks is the result of extensive tinkering with various LAYOUT-related user preferences (see Fig. 5.20) as well as with the *MDU(detailed) Screen*. Many happy hours can be spent running the generator with its endless options until we're satisfied. An efficient way to experiment with these settings is to set "Override Preferences?" to "Y"es on the *Generate Screen*, which allows us to change user preferences on the module level during the generator's dialog (see Section 5.4 above).

Figure 5.20
CASE*Generator for
SQL*Forms User
Preferences Dialog

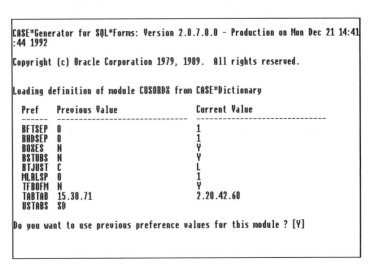

Regarding the design of a form, one detail to note is that blocks and fields cannot be explicitly assigned to pages. This is because CASE*Generator for SQL*Forms calculates the available space depending on the DCU and active user preferences.

We've found it worthwhile to spend time on refining the input for the generator until the desired layout is achieved. This way CASE*Generator for SQL*Forms completely maintains the application. The alternative of changing the layout in SQL*Forms Designer and then **regenerating** the form (for the rest of its existence) results in split maintenance (see end of Appendix B for more on regeneration). The generator then maintains most of its original code (which it has marked), but the developer has to keep close track of every SQL*Forms adjustment.

Our small project doesn't provide a good example for a matrix form, but our client wants to see how one be built, so we've used the relationships between the tables WAREHOUSES, WAREHOUSE_PRODUCTS, and WINE_PRODUCTS to simulate it (see Fig. 5.21). In practice, a form like this would not actually be very useful, but the generator is happy to build it for us (see Section 5.5 on how matrix forms are linked and generated).

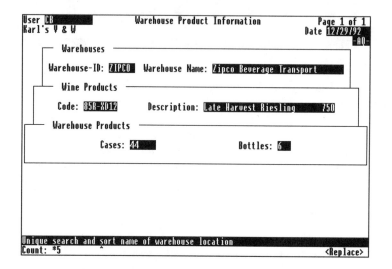

Figure 5.21
Warehouse Product
Information—
a Matrix Form

Another use that clients often want to see demonstrated is a form spanning several pages. Here the context of the "parent and grandparent" of a record are still visible, though they are in different blocks on previous pages (see Figs. 5.22 and 5.23). In our example we explicitly defined the copy context fields on the *MDU (detailed) Screen* by entering "Other = Y" for the detailed column usage of "Description" and "Account Name". Then we used the Override option of the generator to define CONDEP (Context Depth) = 2 and DFTCON (Default Context) = N. Other user preferences used are:

BLKIND (block indentation)	= 2
BSTUBS (block stubs)	= Y
DFTDTE (default date display format)	= MM/DD/YY
CONAME (company name)	= Karl's V & W
PHDMSK (page header date mask)	= MM/DD/YY

Figure 5.22
Order by Account Type
and Account—Page 1

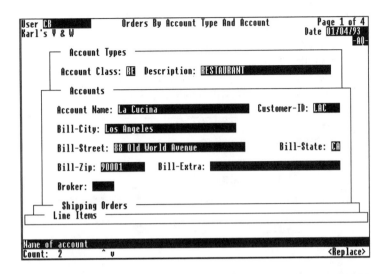

Figure 5.23
Order by Account Type
and Account—with
Copy Context

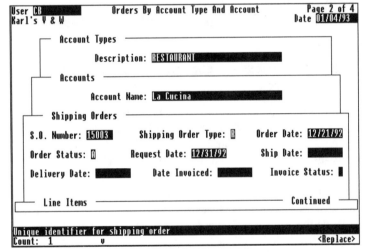

5.8   Designing and Generating a Report

With some experience behind us in CASE*Generator for SQL*Forms, we're ready to begin designing and implementing reports. Since we've already used several of the required tools, the process of creating reports will be easier to learn. In fact, we can start with the *Module Definition Screen* where DAD has provided some report definitions based on our function/ entity specifications. Alternatively, we could define modules here from scratch, a method used for creating ad hoc reports (but beware—any modules defined here for the first time are completely missing from our business analysis models).

It sometimes happens, however, that a user will come up to a developer with a screen shot of a form and say, "This is great. Can you give it to me as a report?" Well, yes we can, by using the

Module Copy Screen (see Fig. 5.24). Here, in the first block, we query for the "Short Name" of the screen module to be duplicated. A new "Short Name" for our copied report module will be inserted in the second block, but this can be overwritten. After we've COMMITted this entry, it's a good idea to return to the *Module Definition Screen* and change the "Language" of our new module to either SQL*ReportWriter or SQL*Plus, depending on the requirements (e.g., a matrix report would be created using SQL*ReportWriter).

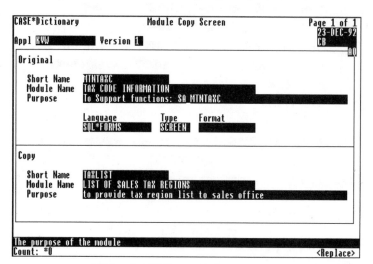

Figure 5.24
Module Copy Screen

No matter how we have defined our report module, the next step is to return to another familiar workplace: the *Module Data Usage (detailed) Screen*. Just as we did with screens, we now need to refine our table and column usages. For example, if we've copied a screen module as a report, all its usages will have been transferred as well. But only the "Select" table usage applies to report modules, and only "Display" usages are valid for columns, so it is best to clean these up here (although the report generator ignores invalid usages after warning us about them). Of course, if we've manually created a report module in the *Module Definition Screen*, we now have to define the detailed table and column usages. Once we have the columns we need with correct usages, their display attributes on page two should also be refined to suit the report's format.

Linking and user preferences, which have a great impact on the design of reports, work just as they do with CASE*Generator for SQL*Forms. As mentioned in Section 5.5, the generator, guided by user preferences, asks us about implicit look-ups. But in our workshop we tend to define links explicitly for the sake of overview and ease of learning. Examining the *Linking between Detailed Table Usages Screen*, we notice that the last column "OJ" (outer join, valid only for nonbase tables) is different from the "Rows" column for screen module linking.

There is one important preference for SQL*ReportWriter that we should mention: DOJOIN. If left at its default "Y"es, the generator will join queries to optimize performance. If "N"o is chosen, the SQL*ReportWriter reports are based on separate queries. In this case, the master rows without details are included—just as with an outer join on a base table. If nothing is entered, the generator will suggest specific queries for joins which can be accepted or rejected.

To generate a basic report module, either in SQL*Plus or with SQL*ReportWriter, we can now proceed to the *CASE*Generator for Reports Screen* (see Fig. 5.25). All the familiar fields are displayed, though in a slightly different sequence. The one obviously new factor (mentioned above) is that now we have two blocks, one for modules generated using SQL*Plus and the other for those using SQL*ReportWriter. Once we press COMMIT from the selected language block, a screen dialog begins that is also very similar to the one for SQL*Forms generation.

Figure 5.25
CASE*Generator for
Reports Screen

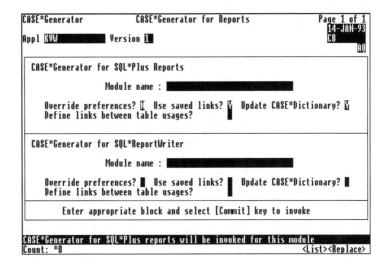

Just as with screen modules, we try to provide as much opportunity as possible for our workshop participants to "play" with the report generator, experimenting with user preferences and column display formats. In keeping with this approach, we'll run through some examples of report types, just to see what CASE*Generator for Reports can do.

5.9   SQL*Plus Reports

When we generate a SQL*Plus report, a command file is created containing SQL and SQL*Plus statements. The documentation at the beginning of this file can be influenced through the DOCFMT preference. (With the user preference SQLONLY=Y, the SQL*Plus formatting commands can be suppressed. This can be very useful if the generated file is to be included, for example, in Oracle Graphics or in a precompiled program.) This command file can be run within the SQL*Plus environment. The only available style for SQL*Plus reports is a tabular format called "CONTROL BREAK" (see Fig. 5.26). Page headers and footers are generated from the module "Top Title" and "Bottom Title" (or the user preference BTITLE). The page size of a report is determined by the WIDTH and HEIGHT preferences, which default to 80 characters by 60 lines. The summary functions AVG, COUNT, MAX, MIN, and SUM are available and can be used at record, group, and/or report level. The output to a file and/or the display of the report on the screen are also determined by user preferences.

```
28-DEC-92                                    Page    1
                   LIST OF SALES TAX REGIONS

Sales Tax Code  Description                   Percentage
--------------  ------------------------------  ----------
0               Not taxable                        .00
CA              Standard California Rate          7.25
CC              Contra Costa County               8.25
LA              Los Angeles County                8.25
SAC             Sacramento County                 7.75
SCL             Santa Clara County                8.25
SF              San Francisco                     8.25

7 rows selected.




*************************************************************************
CASE*Dictionary : Browsing Report File : TAXLIST.lis           (100)
Commands: d,u,l,r,t,b,/(search),n(rep.search),q >>
*************************************************************************
```

Figure 5.26
List of Sales Tax
Regions—a SQL*Plus
Report

A more complex example is displayed in Figure 5.27. The data structure of the report is master/detail but the format is control break. We've generated this SQL*Plus report with the user preference ANDSUM = Y. ANDSUM calculates default summaries for all numeric columns, (which are not part of a primary key), and displays them at group and report level. The other preference used is DTEMSK = MM/DD/YY.

```
01/05/93                                              Page   1
                   ORDERS BY DATE PARAMETERS

S.O.#  Account Name  Date      Code      Description        Qty   Value
------ ------------  --------  --------  -----------------  ----- --------
15003  La Cucina     12/21/92  85R-XD12  Late Harvest         5   760.00
                                         Riesling     750

                     ********                            ----- --------
                     sum                                     5   760.00


15002  La Cucina     12/21/92  85R-XD12  Late Harvest         1   152.00
                                         Riesling     750

                               86CS-D12  Cabernet Sauvignon   2   285.00
                                         750

                     ********                            ----- --------
*************************************************************************
CASE*Dictionary : Browsing Report File : DATORDRS.lis           (79%)
Commands: d,u,l,r,t,b,/(search),n(rep.search),q >>
*************************************************************************
```

Figure 5.27
Orders by Date
Parameters—a SQL*Plus
Report

5.10   SQL*ReportWriter Reports

As an introduction to SQL*ReportWriter reports we simply take the module definitions of our first SQL*Plus report (see Fig. 5.26) and generate it using SQL*ReportWriter instead (see Fig. 5.28). It looks different, doesn't it? By default, SQL*ReportWriter reports have a master/detail format. For the master row, the prompts appear to the left of the field; the detail prompts are on top. Since our simple example doesn't have details it looks a little strange. A more appropriate format to choose would be "CONTROL BREAK", which creates a report very similar to Figure 5.26.

Figure 5.28
List of Sales Tax
Regions—a
SQL*ReportWriter
Report

```
28-DEC-92                                              Page   2 of   3
                        LIST OF SALES TAX REGIONS

Sales Tax Types
---------------
Sales Tax Code: 0           Description: Not taxable

Percentage:    .00


Sales Tax Code: CA          Description: Standard California Rate

Percentage:   7.25


Sales Tax Code: CC          Description: Contra Costa County

Percentage:   8.25


****************************************************************************
CASE*Dictionary : Browsing Report File : TAXLIST.lis              (57%)
Commands: d,u,l,r,t,b,/(search),n(rep.search),q >>
****************************************************************************
```

An Overview of SQL*ReportWriter Objects

As we see in Figure 5.28, the page number is "Page 2 of 3". In addition to the **Report Body**, SQL*ReportWriter reports can have a **Report Title Page** (see Fig. 5.29), followed by **Report Help Text** and a **Report Trailer Page**. These "text objects" are activated by the user preferences TITLEP, HLPTXT, and TRAILP. By default, Title and Trailer Pages are included, but not the Report Help Text, which is entered as module-level User Help Text. So the basic layout of a report is derived from text objects, while the Report Body receives data from one or more queries. Of course, the desired columns are specified on the *MDU (detailed) Screen* and the retrieved rows have to pass the Edit Text validation condition and parameters that a user might enter at run time. Each query produces at least one group that contains the selected columns. In other words, the generator creates a new group for each base table usage and control break (unless a non-breaking column precedes it). A group is a section within a report; for example, summaries may be calculated for it.

We need to create a typical "current orders" list, which provides an ideal example of a master/detail report. This format can be specified on the *Module Definition Screen*. Back at the *MDU (detailed) Screen*, we refine usages so that all necessary tables and columns are present and listed in the order required by the report's format. Then we check to ensure that display types, lengths, and prompts are suitable, especially as regards staying within the specified report width.

```
                 Karl's Vineyard and Winery - Sales


          Report      : LIST OF SALES TAX REGIONS

          Filename    : TAXLIST.lis

          Run by      : C

          Report Date : 01/10/93  02:38pm




**********************************************************************
CASE*Dictionary : Browsing Report File : TAXLIST.lis        (25%)
Commands: d,u,l,r,t,b,/(search),n(rep.search),q >>
**********************************************************************
```

Figure 5.29
SQL*ReportWriter
Title Page

On page three (see Fig. 5.30) we establish the order sequence ("Order Seq") of rows queried from the database and enter required parameter arguments and operators that help determine which data are retrieved. Default values can also be provided for running the report as in Figure 5.31, by using the field "Arg Dflt". Since our client requests the current orders list within a date range, we establish date parameters for the SHIPPING_ORDERS column ORDER_DATE. To do this we create two new usages of ORDER_DATE and enter ">=" as the operator for the argument "startdate" on the first usage and "<=" for "enddate" on the second. Anything entered on page three is automatically added to the table accessed by the *Module Parameter Definition Screen* (see Fig. 5.32).

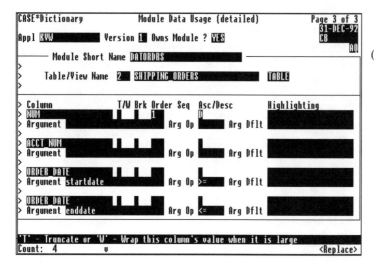

Figure 5.30
Module Data Usage
(detailed) Screen—Page 3

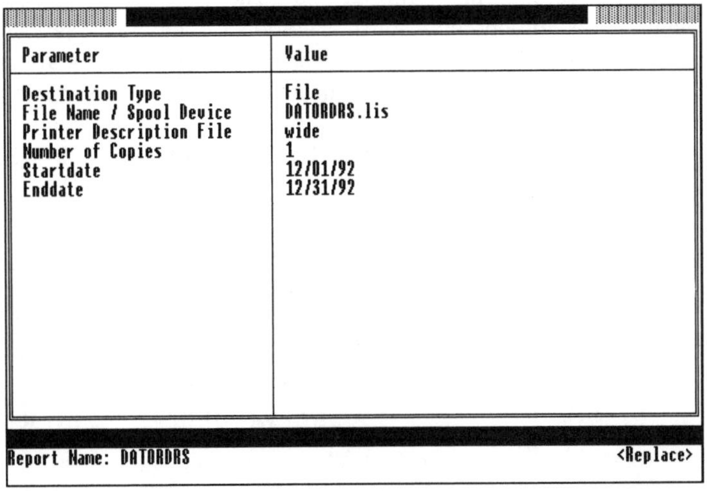

Figure 5.31
SQL*ReportWriter
Parameter Screen

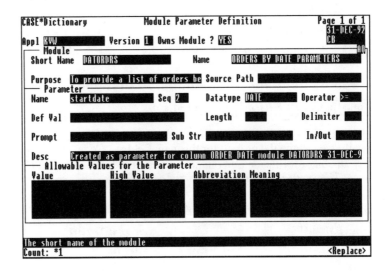

Fig. 5.32
Module Parameter
Definition Screen

The first time we run our master/detail report it has some obvious weaknesses (see Fig. 5.33). First of all, table names are uselessly taking space as group headers. We remove these by deleting the contents of the "Display Title" field under the "Table Name" field in the DTU block of the *MDU (detailed) Screen*. Then there is the problem of width: we want a normal eighty-character-wide format, but we haven't adjusted our prompts and display lengths to achieve that. In fact, we are not even close. Fortunately, we can do it, first by removing a couple of bytes here and there and then by considerably reducing the length of the product code. We decide to format the code as it would appear on a case of wine (an industry standard). To do this we use the *MDU(detailed) Screen*, where we first create a second usage for one of the concatenated primary key columns that forms the code. Then we remove the display usages from all the key columns, leaving only those for the additional usage we've just inserted. After COMMITting these changes, we press [Edit Text] when the cursor is on the row of our added column usage and enter the following expression under the "Derivation Expression" text type:

WINEPRD_YEAR‖WINEPRD_VARIETY‖WINEPRD_STYLE‖

WINEPRD_BOTTLE_SIZE‖WINEPRD_CASE_COUNT

```
┌──────────────────────────────────────────────────────────────────┐
│28-DEC-92                                                           │
│                        LIST OF UNSHIPPED ORDERS                    │
│                                                                    │
│Shipping Orders / Accounts / Account Types                          │
│--------------------------------------------                        │
│Shipping Order Number:   15003          Account Name: La Cucina     │
│                                                                    │
│Class: RESTAURANT                       Order Date: 21-DEC-92   Request│
│                                                                    │
│Order Status: A            Sales Tax Amt:              Freight:     │
│                                                                    │
│   Line Items / Wine Products                                       │
│   --------------------------                                       │
│   Yr  Vty  St  Sz  Ct  Description           Quantity  Unit Price  D│
│   --  ---  --  --  --  ---------------------  --------  ----------   │
│   85  R-   X   D   12  Late Harvest Riesling     750        5    160.00│
│                                                                    │
│                                                                    │
│********************************************************************│
│CASE*Dictionary : Browsing Report File : NEWORDRS.lis       (56%)   │
│Commands: d,u,l,r,t,b,/(search),n(rep.search),q >>                  │
│********************************************************************│
└──────────────────────────────────────────────────────────────────┘
```

Fig. 5.33
List of Unshipped Orders—an SRW Master/Detail Report

Finally we change the prompt for this new field to "Code". Once we've refined some other display attributes for the detail columns, we can produce our report (Fig. 5.34) by setting the user preference DTEMSK to "MM/DD/YY".

```
┌──────────────────────────────────────────────────────────────────┐
│Shipping Order Number:   15002    Account Name: La Cucina           │
│Class: RESTAURANT                       Order Date: 12/21/92        │
│Request Date: 12/22/92     Order Status: A     Sales Tax Amt:       │
│Freight:                                                            │
│                                                                    │
│   Code    Description           Qty  Unit Price  Disc% Line Price  │
│   ------   ----------------------  ---  ----------  ----- ----------│
│   85R-XD12  Late Harvest Riesling   750   1   160.00   5.00   152.00│
│   86CS-D12  Cabernet Sauvignon      750   2   150.00   5.00   285.00│
│                                                    ----------------│
│   Sum                                                      437.00  │
│                                                    ----------------│
│Sum                                                        1197.00  │
│                                                                    │
│                                                                    │
│********************************************************************│
│CASE*Dictionary : Browsing Report File : NEWORDRS.lis       (90%)   │
│Commands: d,u,l,r,t,b,/(search),n(rep.search),q >>                  │
│********************************************************************│
└──────────────────────────────────────────────────────────────────┘
```

Figure 5.34
List of Unshipped Orders—Final Version

Sometimes a report exceeds the available width. Then the generator adds one or more lines to accomodate the overflow. This "wrapping" of lines is not always desirable. The "Multi-Panel" feature of SQL*ReportWriter can be used for master/detail and control break reports. With "MLTPAN = Y", the page overflow is displayed on a separate page.

Figure 5.35
Wine Product
Inventory—a Matrix
Report

```
30-DEC-92                                                       Page   2 of  3
                            WINE PRODUCT INVENTORY

Wines
--------  Warehouses: GILES   GROSKP  KVWHSE  MONVIN PENSA  ZIPCO
84CSRD12              5                444                          449
85R-XD12                     44        150            12     44     250
86CS-D12             76      61        700    45                    882
86R--D12             23      22        1250                         1295
87CS-D12                     95        3578   114     63     88     3938
88SB-D12             128               2212   87      39            2466
                     ------  ------    ------ ------  ------  ------------
                     232     222       8334   246     114    132    9280
                     232     222       8334   246     114    132



**************************************************************************
CASE*Dictionary : Browsing Report File : INVENRPT.lis              (82%)
Commands: d,u,l,r,t,b,/(search),n(rep.search),q >>
**************************************************************************
```

We also want to design and generate a matrix report. We've already developed a matrix form that we duplicate by using the *Module Copy Screen*. On the *Module Definition Screen* we change the "Language" to SQL*ReportWriter and verify that the format is "Matrix". Now we have the basis for a report that formats inventory information, as in Figure 5.35. Note that the sum row for total wine cases by warehouse is repeated. When we defined a second usage for the CASES column as a SUM type on the GROUP level, the first summary row on column and row level was displayed. Then we added a third usage to provide summary data on a REPORT level. This produced the summary column at the bottom far right, as we wanted it, but also added a bottom row that duplicates the group-level sums. The information is, in any case, readable and could be modified in SQL*ReportWriter. Just as with matrix form generation, we link the intersection table to its second master during the dialog. And again, we use the derivation expression above to format the display of our wine product primary key.

As a final example of reports generated using SQL*ReportWriter, we demonstrate a simple list of customer labels (see Fig. 5.36). This can be of interest because the reports generator currently does not implement LABEL-type modules (though "LABEL" is on the module-type list of values). For now we recommend using the RPAD feature to format the names and addresses, as in Figure 5.37. Of course, RPAD can also be used any time we want to format address lines. This derivation expression is defined for a second usage of one of the columns in the address. As with the "Code" example above, the actual base-table columns are defined with nondisplay usages.

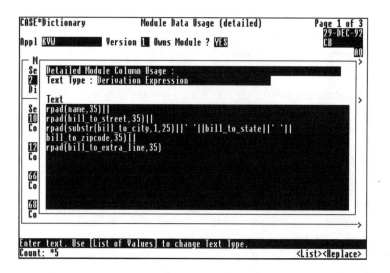

```
Los Angeles CA 90001


Oulala Cuisine
9876 Upscale Parkway
Los Angeles CA 90110


Riskway
99936 Howe Avenue
Sacramento CA 96580


Thelma's Pantry
4455 Nostalgia Boulevard
Los Gatos CA 94332


World Class Distributors
1000 Twin Trade Towers
New York NY 00001
*************************************************************************
  CASE*Dictionary : Browsing Report File : CUSLABEL.lis          (79%)
  Commands: d,u,l,r,t,b,/(search),n(rep.search),q >>
*************************************************************************
```

Figure 5.36
Customer Labels

```
CASE*Dictionary          Module Data Usage (detailed)      Page 1 of 3
                                                           29-DEC-92
Appl KVW          Version 1 Owns Module ? YES              CB
  ┌ M                                                         AO
  │ Se  Detailed Module Column Usage :
  │ 2   Text Type : Derivation Expression
  │ Di
  │     Text
  │ Se  rpad(name,35)||
  │ 10  rpad(bill_to_street,35)||
  │ Co  rpad(substr(bill_to_city,1,25)||' '||bill_to_state||' '||
  │     bill_to_zipcode,35)||
  │ 12  rpad(bill_to_extra_line,35)
  │ Co
  │ 66
  │ Co
  │ 68
  │ Co
  └
Enter text. Use [List of Values] to change Text Type.
Count: #5                                        <List><Replace>
```

Figure 5.37
Derivation Expression
for Customer Labels

5.11 Designing, Generating, and Testing Menus

We now have a substantial array of screen and report modules, but they still need to be related to one another under some kind of superstructure. This is why menus exist: to provide a conveniently accessible path to all the functions within an application. We begin creating our menu structure by proceeding to the *Module Design Utilities Menu* under the *Design Menu* and selecting the *Default Menu System Specification Utility*. Before running this (which is actually just another form of the *Default Application Designer*), we need to be sure that all modules to be included under our menus have been defined and associated to business units. To verify these associations, we check page three of the *Module Definition Screen*. This information has been forwarded from the association of all elementary functions to the business unit SALES that we established during analysis.

Once again, the utility creates candidate modules that we can now accept or delete, this time on the *Candidate Menu Specification Acceptance Screen*. Looking at the result, we note that three menus have been defined: one for report modules and two for screens. We have thirteen screen modules and the user preference MAXOPT (maximum number of options on a menu) has a default setting of ten. So the last three screen modules would be accessed from a third menu. A discussion ensues among our participants on the subject of menu structure. Since we've accepted all candidate menu modules, we turn to the *Module Network Screen* (see the final menu version on Fig. 5.40) to get a better overview of our application. The two options being discussed are 1) to put all screen modules on one menu (MAXOPT = 13) or 2) to refine manually the menu structure. It is decided that we'll take the second route.

But we continue with what we'd be doing in either case: refining menu modules, which means moving to the *Module Definition Screen* where we query on "Type" MENU. There are several different fields here that affect our menu design. For instance, if a user selects a pull-down (see Fig. 5.38) or bar-type menu format, contents of the "Short Title" field (NOT "Short Name"!) will be displayed for the module options. The "Top Title" appears on full-screen menus (see Fig. 5.39), and the "Bottom Title" can be displayed beneath the "Enter your choice" prompt. We need to fill these fields if we don't want substitutes to be chosen for us. In our case, we change some of the top titles and short names of menu modules to provide readable pull-down menu options as well as to conform with the planned restructuring of screen modules beneath them.

Figure 5.38
Orders and Invoicing—
a Pull-down Menu

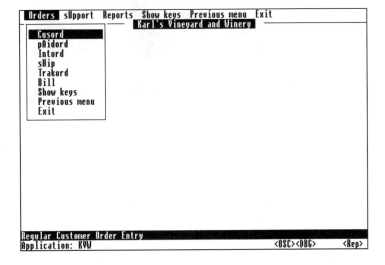

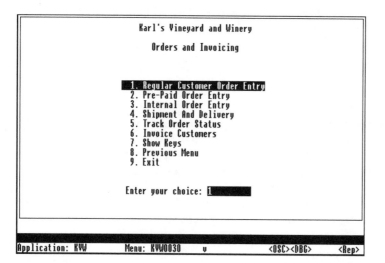

Figure 5.39
Orders and Invoicing—
a Full-screen Menu

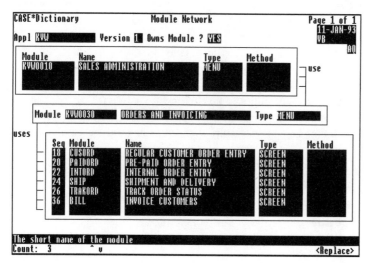

Fig. 5.40
Module Network Screen

The names and titles of our menus are established on the *Module Definition Screen*, but actual re-ordering of the subordinate modules must be done on the *Module Network Screen* (see Fig. 5.40). The middle block on this screen is our "current context." Above this, we see which module is calling the current one and below it, the ones it calls. The [Next Block] key allows us to move into the bottom block where we can delete or insert records. Here we can also resequence the modules as they will appear on the menu, which brings up the issue of good menu design. These are the basic points we stress:

- Order the modules on each menu from top to bottom, from most-used to least-used.

- Keep support table maintenance screens under a separate menu.

- Users don't like too many levels of menus so, as a rule, try to limit the levels to three.

- Don't crowd too many items on one menu.

We use the *Module Network Screen* not only to establish a menu hierarchy or document procedures calling procedures (as in ORACLE7) but also to call a form or a menu from within another form. After defining a connection we need to generate the calling form again so that the appropriate code is created for calling the form or menu and defining a key to get there.

We have finished refining our menu design, so we can proceed to the *CASE*Generator for SQL*Menu Screen*. This is the simplest of all the screens. Only two options are displayed: "Override preferences?" and "Update CASE*Dictionary?". And indeed, though many user preferences are available for it, this is the least complicated of the CASE generators. One useful preference to know is MENSTL: it controls the default menu style. We can choose from FULL-SCREEN, PULL-DOWN, and BAR. But SQL*Menu itself offers additional flexibility here: it allows users to select a menu style for each session by adding an option to their log-on statement.

Once we've generated our menus, we notice the influence of some other user preferences. Looking at Figures 5.38 and 5.39 we see three additional menu options: "Show Keys", "Previous Menu", and "Exit". The appearance of these is governed by the preferences STDSKE, STDPME, and STDEXI. If, for example, we don't want users to be able to exit directly from all menus, we can set STDEXI to "N"o. Something else we notice at the top of our menus is the company title, "Karl's Vineyard and Winery". This is taken directly from the "Title" field of the *Application System Definition Screen*.

Generating menus is an iterative process that most developers find fairly easy to master. Our emphasis in the workshop now shifts to testing the application, and especially to verifying accessibility of modules from the menus.

5.12   Project Delivery

Well, we're nearly finished. It has been a pretty intense two weeks, especially for our hearty participants who have suddenly found themselves in the midst of a powerful new technology. Most of our last day has been devoted to SQL*Menu generation and integration testing, but we finish it off watching our sponsoring user demo the new application for some members of upper management. They seem rather impressed.

5.13   Additional References

For more information on Oracle products, contact Oracle Corporation at (800) 345-DBMS.

To learn more about services provided by the authors, call or write to us at

Renaissance Computer Education and Consulting
P.O. Box 95
Oregon House, CA 95962
(916) 692-2489

Three books have been written specifically on Oracle's CASE*Method:

> Barker, Richard, *CASE*Method, Entity Relationship Modelling*, Addison-Wesley, 1990
>
> Barker, Richard, *CASE*Method, Tasks and Deliverables*, Addison-Wesley, 1990
>
> Barker, Richard and Longman, Cliff, *CASE*Method, Function and Process Modelling*, 1992

There are also quite a few books available on the Oracle tools. One which provides useful information on "upper" CASE (as well as on many other Oracle topics) is Ulka Rodgers's *ORACLE: A Database Developer's Guide* (Prentice Hall, Inc.: Yourdon Press, 1991).

For product-related glossaries of terms, see Oracle's numerous reference guides.

Appendix A

User Extensibility

Oracle allows changes or extensions to its repository, the CASE*Dictionary. This becomes useful in cases where an organization is accustomed to a particular method of managing projects and developing systems, (for example, U.S. government standards). Such an in-house methodology might require that additional elements be stored in the repository. Thus the need to extend CASE*Dictionary arises. This requirement could also come from the wish to integrate tools from different vendors.

The tools and/or techniques involved first need to be analyzed so that concepts specific to them can be identified. This analysis should also define how the new elements will integrate with those already existing in the dictionary. Assuming that the decision has been made to alter the repository, it then needs to be configured so that it can recognize the new elements and their validation rules.

Because extending the repository is work on a "meta-level," Oracle uses the terms *element*, *property*, and *association*. CASE*Dictionary holds data in the form of *elements* such as functions, entities, and modules. These are identified and described by *properties*—for example, the label of a function or the name of an entity. Elements may have *associations* to other elements, e.g., an entity may be associated to a particular function. Oracle allows us to create new elements and associations and to add associations and properties to existing elements by renaming placeholders. For example, "PROPERTY1" becomes "Priority" (see Fig. A.1) if we'd like to store information about the priority of a function.

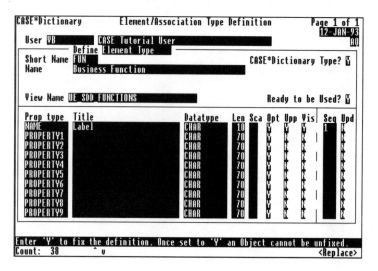

Figure A.1
Element/Association
Type Definition

An outline of steps for implementing User Extensibility follows. This information is intended as an overview—it is not meant to override any of Oracle Corporation's technical bulletins or product documentation.

1. We begin by doing a complete back up of CASE*Dictionary.

2. Then we run the script "cdueins" to install only the extendable CASE definition tables into our private ORACLE account while we continue to share the non-updateable SYSCASE tables in the PUBLIC account.

3. Next we develop our extensions by creating new elements and new associations and/or by adding properties to our previously defined elements or to the standard dictionary Element/Association Types (see Fig. A.1, the *Element/Association Type Definition Screen*).

4. Now we back up our extensions via the *caseexp* utility, preferably as an intermediate user (a little "work-around" currently recommended). To do back ups at every step of this process is time-consuming, but it's the safe way to implement user exensibility.

5. A critical moment has arrived. When the "Ready to be Used" field is set to "Y"es, forms are created that allow data entry for the extended properties. We need to be aware that only limited changes to the extensions are possible, and that deletions are not allowed at all. The only way to get rid of extensions beyond this point is to use a previous back-up copy!

6. So we test our extensions and we test them well until we're really happy with them.

7. But we aren't finished yet. The next step is to create views for the new extensions via the "User Defined Reporter" (see Section 2.11) by running a utility called *Create Reporting Views for User Extensibility* (see Fig. A.2).

8. We verify our extensions by running the *Element Type Definition* and the *Association Type Definition* reports from the *CASE*Dictionary User Extensibility Menu* (see Fig. A.2).

9. After checking out these reports we make our extensions accessible to all CASE*Dictionary users by creating a script that holds the extensions (use "cdueexp"). Now we run it (via "cdueimp") for the user who owns the CASE definition tables (which is, by default, SYSCASE).

10. Finally we clean up by dropping the local definition tables (using the "rmsystab" script).

Two final considerations regarding whether or not to use repository extensibility: 1) Oracle only provides limited support services for your extensions, and 2) dictionaries with different extensions cannot be merged—ever.

Fig. A.2
CASE*Dictionary User
Extensibility Menu

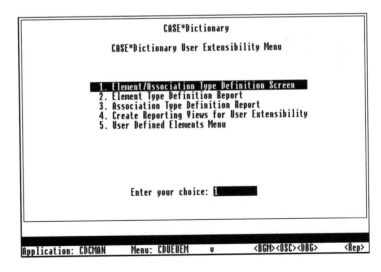

Appendix B
Reverse Engineering and other Re- Words

Anyone who stays abreast of current IS topics will surely have noticed the re- words: reengineering, retrofitting, reverse engineering, re-generating, reconciliation. Let's have a look at how Oracle uses these terms and what CASE can support.

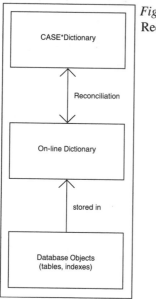

Figure B 1
Reconciliation

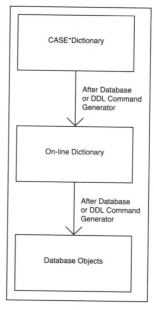

Figure B.2
Changing
On-line Database

Reconciliation means comparing the definitions stored in CASE*Dictionary with the ones in the ORACLE on-line data dictionary. Although ideally they should match exactly at all times, they can become inconsistent. From the *Reconciliation Menu* we select the *Online Dictionary Cross Reference Utility*, which creates a report CDRK.LIS, both listing definitions and pointing at discrepancies.

If we find out that the CASE*Dictionary definitions have been enhanced but that the changes are not yet reflected in the "live" database, the *Alter Database Command Generator* is our tool. It adds columns to a table (see also Section 4.14) and changes their optionality, data type, and size (within the boundaries of the normal ALTER TABLE restrictions). If there are new object definitions in CASE*Dictionary, we use the *DDL Command Generator* as described in Chapter 3 to implement them.

If we discover on-line database objects that have never been documented, we copy them into CASE*Dictionary. This is called **retrofitting** or **reverse engineering of database objects**. The *Reverse Engineer Database Utility* is also accessible from the *Reconciliation Menu*. After the retrofit, we can analyze the existing definitions with all the CASE*Dictionary screens and reports. If there are a few on-line columns that are not documented, we recommend adding them manually on the *Column Definition Screen*.

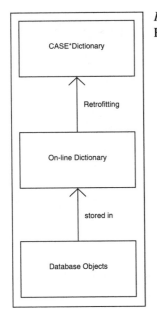

Figure B.3
Retrofitting

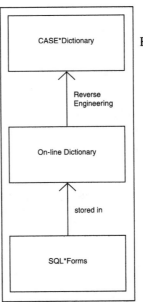

Figure B.4
Reverse
Engineering

CASE*Generator for SQL*Forms is capable of **reverse engineering SQL*Forms applications** stored in the on-line dictionary into module definitions that are, of course, part of the CASE*Dictionary. The *CASE*Generator for SQL*Forms – Reverse Engineer Utility* can be executed from the *CASE*Generator for SQL*Forms Menu*. This is done mainly for documentation purposes, to facilitate impact analysis. However, the stored definitions can also be the basis from which we **re-design** or **re-engineer** forms applications. In a little more detail:

1) A "Module Header" is created with the "Short Name" from the forms name and the "Name" and "Purpose" from the form title or form name. The "Language" is SQL*Forms, the "Type" is SCREEN, the "Format" is MASTER DETAIL, and the "Top Title" is derived from centered text at the top of the form.

2) Module Usages are defined for every base table. We recommend checking the select, insert, and delete flags.

3) On the *Module Data Usage (detailed) Screen*, field characteristics are recorded such as length, format mask, and hint text. The field prompts aren't included.

4) All control blocks and non-base tables are ignored.

5) Summary usages are picked up but again we recommend checking them thoroughly.

Another re- word to define is **re-generate**. *Generating* means creating an application entirely based on CASE*Dictionary information. *Re-generation* is the re-creation of a form that was originally generated from CASE*Dictionary definitions but has since been altered directly in SQL*Forms. For example, changes might have been made in its layout, for tuning purposes, or for the addition of complex triggers. The *CASE*Generator for SQL*Forms – Regenerate Screen* executes this process, which doesn't touch our alterations and still maintains most of its generated code.

Appendix C

Journaling

Let's first clarify what journaling is not: it isn't maintaining a change history column. In cases where, for example, we're interested in knowing when a row is updated and who did it, we can add two columns to our table and use "AG", the automatically generated column values, to populate them with "DM" (date manipulated) and "UM" (user manipulated). Journaling also isn't a systemwide audit where, for example, a DBA might need to enable auditing to monitor successful and/or unsuccessful attempts to connect to the database.

Journaling means keeping track of a table's history. A journal table records all inserts, updates, and deletes of the table it accompanies. It's quite easy to implement (as described below) but before we do, we need to think deeply about its impact on the performance of our forms and the size of our database. Every time a row is inserted, updated, or deleted, both the original and the journal table have to be accessed. On insert and update, the data row is written into the journal table, which grows rather quickly if there are many DML operations. Whenever the user deletes a row, only the primary key values are recorded together with the journal information (see Fig. C.1).

```
JN_ JN_ORACLE_USER              JN_DATETI
--- --------------------------- ---------
JN_NOTES
--------------------------------------------------------------------------
JN_APPLN                        JN_SESSION COD DESCRIPTION
--------------------------------- ---------- --- ----------------------------
PERCENTAGE
----------
INS CB                              21-DEC-92

MTNTAXC                                    MRN Marin County
        7.75

UPD CB                              21-DEC-92
Incorrect percentage previously entered.
MTNTAXC                                    MRN Marin County
        8

DEL CB                              22-DEC-92

MTNTAXC                                    MRN

SQL>
```

Figure C.1
Displaying Journal Table
in SQL*Plus

If we know during data design that a journal table will be needed, we simply enter "Journal Table = Y" on the *Table Definition Screen.* No other steps are required, though we'd strongly recommend using a non-updatable primary key. The following is a series of steps to take when we discover the need for a journal table late in the development process:

1. Create the journal table definitions by setting the field "Journal Table" to "Y" on the *Table Definition Screen.*

2. Create the journal table itself by running the DDL Command Generator for the table to be journaled. We can edit the script CDCDDL.SQL to remove the invalid CREATE TABLE statement for the table being journaled before we run the script.

   As shown in Figure C.2, the journal table has the name of the original table with "_JN" appended to it. Besides all the original columns, it contains six additional ones for:

Figure C.2
Creating a Journal Table

```
CREATE TABLE SALES_TAX_TYPES_JN (
    JN_OPERATION              CHAR(3)         NOT NULL,
    JN_ORACLE_USER            CHAR(30)        NOT NULL,
    JN_DATETIME               DATE            NOT NULL,
    JN_NOTES                  CHAR(240)       NULL,
    JN_APPLN                  CHAR(30)        NULL,
    JN_SESSION                NUMBER(38)      NULL,
    code                      CHAR(3)         NOT NULL,
    description               CHAR(30)        NULL,
    percentage                NUMBER(4,2)     NULL
)
PCTFREE        0
;

COMMENT ON TABLE SALES_TAX_TYPES_JN
IS 'Journal table for sales_tax_types' ;

PROMPT Adding PRIMARY Constraint To SALES_TAX_TYPES Table

ALTER TABLE SALES_TAX_TYPES ADD (
    PRIMARY KEY (CODE)
*****************************************************************
CASE*Dictionary : Browsing Report File : cdcddl.sql          (96%)
Commands: d,u,l,r,t,b,/(search),n(rep.search),q >>
*****************************************************************
```

- the operation performed (INS, UPD, DEL)

- the ORACLE user who did it

- Date and time of the transaction (set the user preference WHTIME to record the time)

- Notes or a reason for this transaction (the user preferences JNNTRG and JNNTMD allow/enforce the user to enter a reason for a particular operation—see Fig. C.3)

Figure C.3
Tax Code Information
with Journal
Column "Reason"

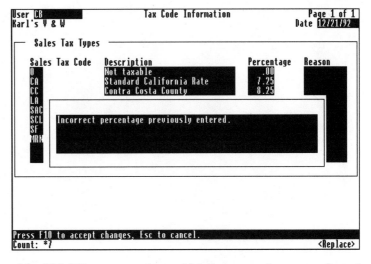

- the name of the SQL*Forms screen from which the transaction was performed

- the session identifier (set the user preference JNSSID)

3. Generate the module again so that CASE*Generator for SQL*Forms can write all code to support journaling. Figure C.2 shows the JN_NOTES or "Reason" field with its display length of ten characters and its actual length of 240 characters (invoked by pressing the [Edit] key).

During the workshop one team member has noticed that she cannot query a journal table separately on the *Table Definition Screen*. Neither do we have access to the JN_NOTES field on the *MDU (detailed) Screen*. Through SQL*Plus we can look at the entire journal table (see Fig. C.1). To use it for customized reports we recommend retrofitting it into CASE*Dictionary.

Appendix D

Diagrams

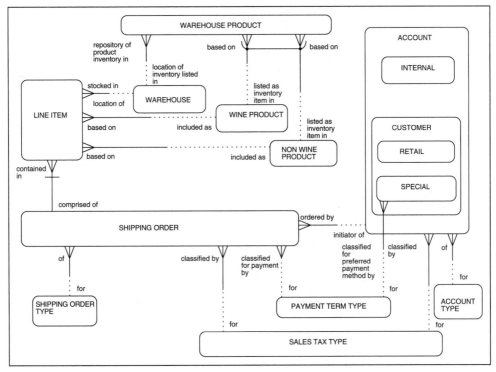

Figure D.1 Final Workshop ERD

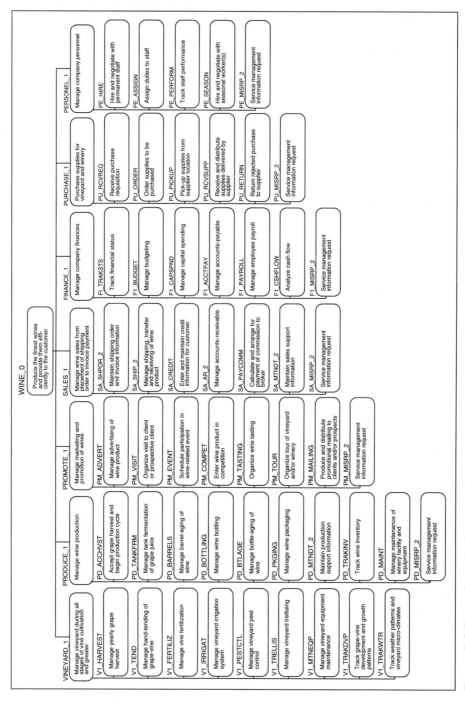

Figure D.2 Enterprise-wide Function Hierarchy

Appendix E

List of Figures

125